More Time To Think

More Time To Think

The Power Of Independent Thinking

Nancy Kline

CASSELL ILLUSTRATED

An Hachette UK company
www.hachette.co.uk

First published in Great Britain in 2009 by
Fisher King Publishing

This edition published in 2015 by
Cassell, a division of Octopus Publishing Group Ltd
Carmelite House
50 Victoria Embankment
London EC4Y 0DZ
www.octopusbooks.co.uk
www.octopusbooksusa.com

Distributed in the US by
Hachette Book Group
1290 Avenue of the Americas
4th and 5th Floors
New York, NY 10020

Distributed in Canada by
Canadian Manda Group
664 Annette St.
Toronto, Ontario, Canada M6S 2C8

ISBN 978-1-84403-796-4

A CIP catalogue record for this book is available
from the British Library.

Printed and bound in the United States by
RR Donnelley

10 9 8 7 6 5 4 3 2

Publisher: Denise Bates
Deputy Art Director: Yasia Williams-Leedham
Design: Jeremy Tilston
Graphic illustrations: Tim Barnes
Production Controller: Sarah Kramer

For Merl

... the most

In Memoriam

Margaret Legum

Pioneer

Liberator

Friend

Contents

Acknowledgements

The without-whoms are numerous. And they reach across to many others, and soon we touch my parents, and then theirs, and then theirs, until, logically, we end up with the particles just after the big bang. So, this will be the short version.

Some people in life, contrary to accepted wisdom, are irreplaceable. Stephanie Archer, in the development of Time To Think and in the completion and publication of this book, is one. As far as I am concerned, whatever good I did in my life for the first 56 years allowed me to merit meeting Stephanie.

Christopher Spence, my husband and key advisor, is in every word of this book. His experience in pioneering and creating Thinking Environments as a Chief Executive for more than 20 years, his being a Thinking Environment in all of his relationships, (most especially ours), and his believing both in the Thinking Environment and in me permeate the pages here. I thank him also for his invaluable reading and editing of the manuscript.

If it were not for Vanessa Helps, I might still be stuck on the first paragraph. Unable to begin, I began instead a letter to Vanessa, my friend and co-coach. As I wrote to her, the book broke through. And the letter became my *Vanessa Journal* to start each day, and to get past each impasse.

Along the way these people made a specific difference: Beth Black encouraged the very first draft; and Laura Meadors Johnson welcomed my letters about it, so that six years later my voice could find itself.

Paul Gregory's coaching brought me back into the right relationship with the book. Scott Farnsworth inveigled me and picked up my pace by publishing two books himself in the same amount of time. Jez Cartwright focused me positively on best publishing options. Simon Hewat helped me distinguish between the prestige of dinosaurs and the integrity of the cutting edge. Gilly Glyn and Ruth McCarthy liberated the back cover. Rob Brown inspired the title, and the publisher. Trisha Lord offered me a life-changing gift.

Then there is the Time To Think Collegiate, the 79 qualified Time To Think Facilitators, Coaches and Consultants across four continents. From our learning, discovering, refining and thinking together, this book takes its authority, and I take the greatest joy.

What is the purpose of life? he asked.
To be yourself, she answered.
But aren't I already myself? he asked.
You are now, she answered.
But people over six usually aren't.
Why is that? he asked.
Because when they are little,
no one ever asks them what they think.

Introduction

When I was 17, I discovered a wonderful thing. My father and I were sitting on the floor of his study. We were organizing his old papers. Across the carpet I saw a fat paper clip. Its rust dusted the cover sheet of a report of some kind. I picked it up. I started to read. Then I started to cry.

It was a speech he had written in 1920, in Tennessee. Then only 17 himself and graduating from high school, he had called for equality for African Americans. I marvelled, proud of him, and wondered how, in 1920, so young, so white, and in the deep South, where the law still segregated black from white, he had had the courage to deliver it.

"Daddy," I said, handing him the pages, "this speech – how did you ever get permission to give it? And weren't you scared?"

"Well, honey," he said, "I didn't ask for permission. I just asked myself, 'What is the most important challenge facing my generation?' I knew immediately.

"Then I asked myself, 'And if I weren't afraid, what would I say about it in this speech?'

"I wrote it. And I delivered it. About half way through I looked out to see the entire audience of faculty, students and parents stand up – and walk out. Left alone on the stage, I thought to myself, 'Well, I guess I need to be sure to do only two things with my life: keep thinking for myself, and not get killed.' "

He handed the speech back to me, and smiled. "I seem to have done both," he said.

"Thank you," I said.

I had no idea then just how much I was thanking him for. I knew he had set aside fear to be a person of conviction. That was plenty. But he had also been a person thinking for himself by asking powerful questions and listening to the answers.

I learned courage and integrity from him that day. But I also learned that doing your own thinking is the first step in making a difference.

That day was one juncture in a journey that would eventually unfold as Time To Think and its work, The Thinking Environment.

The Context

I think that we are living in an epidemic of obedience. I think also that we are developing sophisticated victims in our leaders and executives.

If we could count them, I believe we would find that most people making decisions, even at the very top, are going along with, in effect obeying, the people who pay them. The crises we face today started with obedience yesterday. And the decisions that led to the crises were made by people who were paid well to carry out someone else's, even some system's, wishes. Who, we might well ask, is thinking?

I ponder what it will take to produce a planet of people thinking for themselves – in the best interest of all people. Turning our organizations and governments and religions and schools and families into Thinking Environments may be part of it. It will surely be, I think, if in our hearts we want the best for each other. I believe that we do. I believe that we are not kidding about this.

And I believe that we are brave enough to stop the epidemic and free the victims. Somewhere we know we are this good.

The Provenance

This Thinking Environment has emerged from one important observation and one importunate question. The observation is simple. It is even a bit dry. But it is chilling in its implications. It can slip right by us if we are not looking. And the price we pay for not seeing it is high. The observation is:

> The quality of everything human beings do, everything –
> everything – depends on the quality of the *thinking* we
> do first.

If this observation is true, and I think it is almost certain (although I am wary of certainty – I think it is a drug, and an impossibility), it changes our understanding of leadership. It places right at the top of required expertise in leaders and professionals and parents and teachers the ability to generate people's finest independent thinking.

Suddenly then, in the horizon emerges this question:

> How do we help people to think for themselves, with
> rigour, imagination, courage and grace?

How do we do that?

That question has fascinated me for most of my life. You may know from the first book, *Time To Think: Listening To Ignite The Human Mind*, that in 1973 Peter Kline and I founded Thornton Friends School and began to look for answers to that question.

Over the years we and our colleagues confirmed that the most important factor in whether or not people can think for themselves is *how they are being treated by the people with them while they are thinking.*

The way people *behave* with each other actually determines the quality of their *thinking*. Behaviour in the listener is more important than IQ, education, experience or background in the thinker.

Over time we noticed that there were ten behaviours that enhance people's thinking most. (I am sorry there are ten; it seems too pat, and disturbingly biblical. Maybe you will discover an eleventh. If you do, we will un-neaten the list in a flash.)

We began to see that the Ten Components of a Thinking Environment are around us all of the time, darting in and out of view, igniting people's thinking, but intermittently crashing into other behaviours that inhibit people's thinking. We had to extricate the thinking-enhancing behaviours from the thinking-inhibiting ones. As we did, we could see that their power was undeniable.

No archaeologists were ever more exhilarated than we were, after years of digging, to gaze upon that simple fact.

If we behave in ten particular ways, people around us will think for themselves, often brilliantly.

The Wide Applicability

I went on in 1985 to explore whether the Ten Components would appear consistently in other settings as well. Would business executives or scientists or coaches or musicians or healthcare professionals or lawyers or parents find those behaviours as powerful as we had in the classroom?

Yes.

In fact, the wide applicability of the Thinking Environment has astounded me. Corporate teams, a country's president, nurses, estate-planning lawyers, partners, writers, engineers, executive coaches, golf champions, siblings, mediators, HR professionals, teachers, project managers, facilitators, sexual health practitioners, youth workers, sports teams, leaders for a non-racist world, secretaries, architects, pilots are embracing this way of being with people.

When people use these processes to decide, to create, to coach, to mentor, to chair meetings, to teach, to develop policy, to re-structure organizations, to design products, to build family life, to market, to strategise, to debate, to mediate, to start their day, to love, they bring into being a lissom thinking culture.

The Results

And the reported results are impressive. The most profound ones have been soft ones, human ones. They are big things like dignity, swellings of motivation, deepening of commitment, preference for collaboration, improved performance, and the creative release that comes from knowing irrevocably that you matter.

I think this is because by its nature, the Thinking Environment welcomes people. It gives them permission to be as intelligent, as imaginative, as kind, as rigorous, as inspiring, as indefatigable as they, at their core, truly are.

But, as if this were not enough, we have seen the metrics match the magic. The important soft results are proving to produce hard, measurable ones, too. Like these:

The President of Zambia saved 40% of the GNP in 36 minutes.

A company rescued a $200,000,000 product in 45 minutes.

15 senior officers, from 11 organizations across 3 continents, consistently transformed ineffective, time-wasting meetings into generative and productive time of significant value to the organization and its people.

A financial services company measured a 20%+ business improvement across the board by developing the Thinking Environment as their meetings culture.

A government agency saved 62% of senior management time over 6 months.

A hospital moved in nine months from one star to four.

A telecommunications company saved 30 days of work in 40 minutes.

A national golf team won the world championship for the first time.

A medical team saved 44% of the cost of each decision.

And there has been another, surprising result. The Thinking Environment seems to create time. I did not expect this. It was enough for me that the Thinking Environment can liberate the human mind. Finding that it also generates time was a bonus. In most lives time to think is critically needed and criminally scarce. Time gained, it seems to me, calls for near jubilation.

The results resound.

The Simplicity

But I am most impressed by the simplicity of the Thinking Environment. The Ten Components, with one exception, are simple. They are even familiar. Learning them, we are not winded by impenetrability. We take them in and recognize them immediately. And that amazes me. I have always assumed that for something to further our understanding of thinking, it would have to be complex and esoteric, like Epistemology or String Theory.

But the Components of a Thinking Environment are straightforward and open-hearted and comprehensible. People, in fact, continue to marvel that such a simple process produces such stunning results.

That doesn't make the Ten Components easy to master, however, because they are almost the opposite of what our teachers teach and our professionals profess. And so they can at first seem difficult. But they are simple. And soon they become a joy. And former ways of behaving with each other become anathema.

This book is the next instalment in the story of human beings treating each other so well they generate superb thinking in each other. Lives change as a result. And hearts thrive. And futures reshape themselves for good.

The Book

The book is in four parts.

PART ONE: IN THEORY tells you more about the Positive Philosophical Choice, a view of life and of human nature that frees the human mind. This part also considers the importance of being willing to be wrong in order to get closer to being right. And it takes you into our new understandings of the depth, detail and long, elegant sweep of the Ten Components.

PART TWO: IN PRACTICE tells you in two sections more about the dynamic applications of the Ten Components.

> IN PAIRS includes The Thinking Partnership, Dialogue, Coaching, Coach Supervision, Mentoring and Mediation.

> IN GROUPS includes Transforming Meetings, The Time To Think Council, Facilitation and Speaking with Authenticity.

PART THREE: IN PROGRESS tells you the story of five forays into change that people are making around the world, using the Thinking Environment. The variety of focus includes: sustainability and The Sign of Enough, values, legacy, email, the internet and cultural transformation.

PART FOUR: IN THE END is a consideration of paradox, of its permeation of the Thinking Environment and its central role in generating successful independent thinking. We ponder paradox in two poems: one by TS Eliot, one by Davison Budhoo, both analogies for moments of independent thinking.

THE APPENDIX is a dip into two research studies of the Thinking Environment, and a look at seven powerful questions.

THE BIBLIOGRAPHY leads you to readable writing about the human mind and its wonders.

Throughout, the book proposes that creating a Thinking Environment everywhere all of the time is a worthy goal. And, like peace, it contains within itself a fine strategy to get us there.

Throughout the book as well is the quiet injunction for us to make a re-iterative decision to *live* these Ten Components. I continue to be grateful to Shirley Edwards who said it well:

> The Thinking Environment is not a set of techniques. It is
> a way of being in the world.

She also understood that the Ten Components require us to use unusual rigour in order to achieve unprecedented results.

They require us to fall headlong into the vast potential of the human mind, and into each other's most deeply held dreams for a world that works well for everyone.

As you read on, consider this: in whatever time is left in your life, through whatever work you do or lives you influence, you can choose, minute to minute, to make a difference. You may want to do this through the creation of new organizational policy or technology. But those achievements will be subject to changes by the politics, economics, innovations and ambition of others who emerge after you are gone.

But the Thinking Environment expertise you instil will be carried like seed through every life that touches other lives, and through the gradually increasing quality of thinking and culture that results.

I invite you to ponder the possibilities. That is, if you can bear the beauty.

The Ten Components Of A Thinking Environment

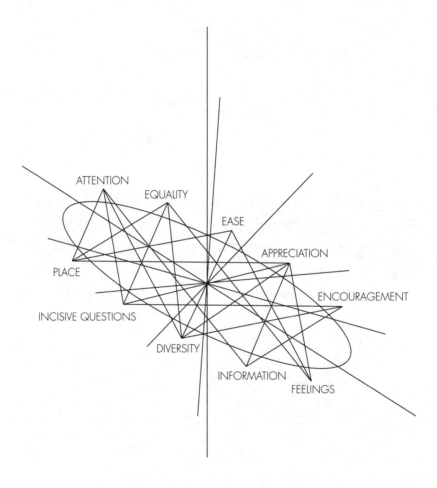

Part One

In Theory

CHAPTER 1

What Do You Think?

"Do you know what happens," Martin asked me, "when a Third World country loses 40 percent of its revenue overnight?"

I listened.

"Within a few weeks food disappears from shelves. Essential drugs in hospitals deplete. Well people get sick, and sick people die. Petrol runs out. Buses stop running. Children don't go to school. Civil servants don't get paid. Soon police cannot control the contractions of violence. And when 40 percent of your nation's money comes from other nations, it can disappear overnight.

"That was the situation in Zambia, my country," he continued.

I continued to listen.

"But," Martin said, "the story begins a year before when President Mwanawasa was elected. I wanted him to know what makes good leadership. Defying my fear, I decided to telephone him."

I wanted to say, "Wow, can someone just call a President?" But I restrained myself. Martin went on.

"I rang State House. 'This is Martin Kalungu-Banda,' I said. 'May I speak to the President, please?'

"'Is he expecting your call?' the voice said.

"'No, but I have a very important message for him.'

"'Hold on,' the voice said.

"'Hello?' said the next voice. 'What is it you want, please?'

"'I am Martin Kalungu-Banda, and I want to speak to the President.'

"'That is not possible without an appointment. Can you tell me the nature of this?'

"'No, I said, 'I need to speak directly to the President.'

"'That won't be possible.'

"Again, I was on hold. I waited.

"Then yet another voice came on.

"'Yes, how can I help you?'

"Feeling impatient I replied, 'I am requesting to speak to the President.'

"'You are speaking to the President,' the new voice said.

"My heart pounded. I adjusted my posture on the chair. My voice trembled. I said, 'Mr. President. I did not vote for you, but I would like to share with you what I have been learning about leadership. How possible is it to meet with you, Sir?'

"The President said nothing. Neither did I.

"My heart pounded harder.

"'At least you were honest about your vote,' the President joked. He paused. 'I would be delighted to hear what you are learning. Today is Tuesday. Can you make it this Friday at 15:00 hours?'

"'Yes, thank you, Sir,' I said, believing and disbelieving what I had just heard.

"On Friday, standing in front of him, I gathered my thoughts. I looked straight into his eyes. I said, 'Sir, if you want your presidency to succeed, you will need to do one thing for the people. Just one.'

"'And what is that, Martin?' he asked, truly listening.

"'Serve,' I said.

"'Serve?' the President asked.

"'Yes,' I said. 'Serve.'

"'That's it?' he asked.

"'Yes,' I repeated.

"'You must see yourself as the people's servant.'

"I stopped, not sure where I would go from there.

"The President smiled. He leaned back in his chair. He was quiet.

"Then he said slowly, 'Well, Martin Kalungu-Banda, I have no idea how I would do that.' He paused. He leaned forward.

"'Maybe you will just have to teach me.'

"I could not take it in.

"'Please come to my home for dinner tomorrow evening,' he continued.

"The next evening we talked until nearly midnight. The President took notes. He listened. He took more notes. Then he said, 'Martin, even if I were to apply the servant leadership model to governing, it would not work unless all of my colleagues practise it, too.' My heart started up again. I feared the worst.

"But he surprised me.

"'Can you conduct a leadership workshop for the Cabinet?' he asked.

Martin's initiative and courage were quickly raising the bar for my own life.

Martin continued. "The reason I am telling you this story, Nancy, is that for some reason the President trusted me. And a year later he asked me to become his Special Consultant.

"Before I left for that job, a colleague said to me, 'Martin, you may need this in your new post.' And she handed me your book.

"I read it, and I kept it close to me.

"And one day I used part of it to help the President save the country.

"This is what happened," he continued. "The President had fired the Director of the Anti-corruption Commission. He was planning to appoint a better man.

"But he refused to inform the western diplomats about this plan. They said that they would withdraw their funds (40 percent of our revenue) if the government did not re-instate the Director by Monday. It was Friday.

"'Martin, I will not allow diplomats to rule this country from behind the scenes,' the President insisted.

"I began to worry. Then I began to panic. The prospect of 40 percent of national revenue disappearing within 3 days was terrifying. And real.

"I felt I could not push my point further. I thanked him and left.

"Through the night I worried about what would happen on Monday morning.

"I gathered courage. I called the President at his home.

"'Your Excellency,' I said, 'the donors need to know that you are committed to anti-corruption. Can we maintain our sovereignty and still inform the donors? Is there room, Sir, to do both?'

"The President was quiet. Then he reached for the phone. 'Please call all the diplomats to a meeting with me on Monday before noon,' he said to his secretary.

"On Monday morning early I met with the President.

"I went back in my mind to page 102 of *Time To Think*.

"I said, 'Sir, my suggestion is that when you open the meeting, you immediately enable each diplomat to put his voice into the room. You could do this by asking them a question of some sort, and then give everyone a turn in a Round to speak without interruption. And that would mean you would not interrupt either, Sir.'

"'Then you could appreciate the support they have been giving.

"'And you could, Sir, then reiterate your unwavering commitment to fighting corruption. You could tell them there will be a new Director of the Commission.'

"He was listening intently.

"I continued. 'Sir, you could ask: What do you think, and what questions do you have?

"'Then after everyone has spoken, you could respond as appropriate.

"'Then you could ask each person what closing thoughts they have.'

"Again my heart was pounding.

"The President was quiet. He looked at his notes.

"He looked up. 'This plan sounds good,' he said, 'and I think *you* should manage the meeting, Martin.'

"'With all due respect, Sir, I think the entire meeting should come from you. It will have far more impact.'

"He nodded. 'Then I need to think about this myself,' he said.

"I left the office.

"At 11am sharp the President and I entered the meeting room. After welcoming everyone, the President asked, 'What issues are keeping you busy?'

"'A great question,' I thought. And I was impressed by his conducting of the Round.

"He then told them about the new Director, and when he asked the diplomats what they thought or wanted to say, the first diplomat said, 'Your Excellency, we are very grateful that you have chosen to inform us about your decision. We know, Sir, that we are not entitled to this kind of treatment, but we interpret it as a show of your confidence in our being co-operating partners with your government. We also applaud the changes you are making. And I confirm our support to your country.'

"Every diplomat expressed a similar view.

"The President concluded by asking each person what further thoughts they had. He then thanked everyone, and we left. We walked down the long corridor, and when we were out of ear shot of the group, he opened his arms and said in a loud whisper, jubilant, 'Martin, it worked!'

"'Yes,' I said. I paused. 'If you do it just that way, it seems to.'

Martin and I looked at each other. He was radiant.

"And, Nancy," he said, beaming, "that took only 36 minutes!"

We laughed together.

He looked out through the glass and across the large open space of desks. Then he looked back at me.

"It is simple, isn't it?" he said.

I nodded, and smiled.

"I guess most profound things are."

CHAPTER 2

What Is The Secret?

The Ten Components Of A Thinking Environment

What happened that morning with Martin and the President? How were they able to save their country? Was it because all of the Ten Components of a Thinking Environment were present? Is that also why it took only 36 minutes?

I think so.

These Ten Components, these ten ways of being with each other, are a creative force. They generate good thinking in people. They generate open-mindedness toward each other. They create safety and trust. And thus they elicit people's authentic selves. They dignify people. They help people to be at ease around others so that breakthrough thinking can flow between them.

It is from that quality of thinking that people make the best decisions.

And I think, even after exploring these Ten Components for years, we are only just beginning to know them.

Individually

One thing we do know about them is that, individually, each Component improves people's thinking. If you offer only one of these Components, the person with you will think better.

If you give Attention of generative quality, born of deep interest in what the person thinks and will say next, they will think better around you than they will if you interrupt them or listen only in order to reply.

If you regard the person thinking as your thinking Equal, regardless of any power differential between you, they will think better around you than if you see yourself as better than (or less than) they are.

If you are at Ease *inside yourself*, regardless of the degree of (mostly manufactured) urgency and rush outside you, people will think better (and faster) around you than if you are in a hurry yourself.

If you genuinely Appreciate people five times more than you criticize them, they will think more clearly and imaginatively around you than if you focus on their faults.

If you Encourage people – build with them their courage to go to the unexplored edge of their thinking by championing their excellence – they will think better around you than if you compete with them.

If you offer accurate and complete Information to people, and if you show respect for their facing what they have been denying, they will think better around you than if you collude with their assumption that what is true is not true, or that what is not true, is.

If you welcome the expression of people's Feelings and are relaxed in the face of their tears or anger or fear, they will think better around you than if you race to in some way anaesthetize them.

If you are interested in the Diversity between you and others, the differences both in your ideas and in your group identities and cultures, they will think better around you than if you indicate, however subtly, that being just like you is best.

If you can ask people an Incisive Question, one that replaces an untrue limiting assumption with a true, liberating one, they will think better around you than if you abandon them to limiting assumptions.

And if you can prepare the Place where you and they think together so that it says to them, "You matter," they will think better around you than if you allow the place to be intimidating, inaccessible or culturally and aesthetically barren.

Any one of these Ten Components of a Thinking Environment is capable of improving people's thinking. And people are grateful for any one of them any chance they get.

All Ten At Once

But in fact the Components call out to each other. Each needs the others to be fully itself. Life is like that, isn't it? Nothing can be understood in isolation. If we seek to understand one thing without considering it in relationship, what we understand will not truly be it. (However, the impossibility and absurdity of compartmentalization has never stopped human beings from doing it with impunity.) So, if you can embody all ten of these behaviours at once, as a kind of system, people's thinking can become transformative. All Ten Components experienced at once create a culture of superb thinking and graceful human connection.

In this part of the book, we will immerse ourselves in these Components. The stories they tell are testimony to their impact. And to the importance of our getting very, very good at them.

The Components also form the theoretical backbone of the Thinking Environment. They then lead us immediately to action. Because, as Margaret Legum taught me, there is nothing more practical than a good theory.

Let's start with possibly the most important Component, the one that is, in itself, an act of creation.

CHAPTER 3

Who Is The Creator?

Attention

Listening without interruption

Being interested in what the person will say next

Attention is an act of creation

Listening to reply is different from listening to ignite

As the thinker, knowing you will not be interrupted frees you truly to think for yourself

Three weeks before my twin brother died, he said many things I am still pondering and that I shall always treasure. He and I had been sitting in silence. I was taking in his serenity and sweetness as it penetrated my still robust unwillingness to acknowledge that these days were last days. He was just being, honouring the moment, honouring me, honouring life.

Then out of the silence, out of the blue, blue as in infinity, he said carefully and clearly. "When you love him, you get to listen, and then...."

I waited. This life in front of me was a whole world.

"And then, you get to listen, more and more."

He smiled. He drifted.

I burned those words into my brain, wanting to protect them from the busy tumour in his. They mattered. I understood them fully, and also not at all.

For him those words were probably about God. Knowing him, I am sure they were, in fact. But I thought, knowing Bill, that they were also about people. Those words were a principle of the universe, simple, blinding. And thus easily missed.

In fact, in that moment I knew that most of what I had been observing, researching, teaching, lecturing about for nearly 30 years, the whole of the Thinking Environment and the books I had written about it, were alive in those stunning 17 words. (Why can't a work be just 17 words long and leave it at that?)

If I could have, I would have asked Bill whether he meant that when we love people, that is, when we respect them as human beings, as thinkers, our love – our respect – sets up the conditions for them to say the true things, the real things, to face the barriers, to understand them, to banish them, to see the possibilities, to discover how to get there, to do, in other words, their own thinking. And being present for that is a gift to us, the listeners. To be present for that, to help make that happen, is a privilege.

I am sure he would have agreed and smiled again, amused by my need to pick apart and understand what for him was bestowed mystery. "Yes," he might have said, "that is one reason why when we love him, we get to listen."

Listening like this is conception. It is a creative force. And it is a paradox. It is creator, and it is creation. It is the sending of seed, and it is the soil. I am sure that only physicists and poets understand this kind of impossibility: the genius of opposites. The faces and the vase. One and both, at once.

Most people have no idea how to generate Attention like this. Most people think that listening is linear. They think that listening is lined up waiting, waiting to speak.

They think that listening is their impatient not-doing until they finally can do. Most people watch for the holes, the pause, the intake of breath, the looking off into sky, the slightest flutter of being finished, so that, finally, they can speak.

Most people miss the creator. Most people miss the ignition that is inside the listening.

This is because listening this profoundly can feel like just sitting there.

It can feel like not being an expert. It can feel like not being a leader. It can feel like doing nothing. It can feel like a waste of time.

But Attention of this calibre is exactly the thing that saves time, that even generates time.

This is because truly good independent thinking emerges. It is not hammered or sculpted. It comes *from*. It stands ready, and when you are ready, it floats from some cool ground. A person's finest thinking lives inside those linings of minutes when you are not plotting or trying or prying loose.

These moments of the person's mind re-connecting with its own power take your breath away, and you wonder how you could ever have wanted them to look to you for the answers. As you listen, you can touch, and sometimes be filled to the top, by the beauty in front of you.

This happens because you are comfortable with the paradoxes. You understand that, as the catalyst for this fine thinking, you are both essential and irrelevant. You matter profoundly, because you do not matter at all.

In both a conceptual and chemical sense, Attention like this is a catalyst. Take that word out of common parlance for a moment and let it transport you. A catalyst in biochemistry is an amazing thing. It is a substance that increases the rate of a change without being consumed or changed itself. A catalyst also lowers the energy required for the change, allowing the change to proceed more quickly or at a lower temperature.

This is what Attention does. It brings about change in a person's thinking by firing up connections and leaps and divings. And, like a catalyst, this Attention is constant. It is not changed by what the thinker does. And so it is a steady resource for them. They can count on this Attention to hold fast, to be intelligent, unconfused, compassionate, unconsumed and unchanged by where their thinking is going.

Attention in that way allows their thinking, their changing, to proceed more quickly and with less energy. Chemical catalysts can accelerate change up to a factor of 1,020. I suspect Attention's accelerating of change in human thinking is far faster.

Attention of this quality recognizes that *listening to reply is different from listening to ignite*. Most people, including most professionals, listen to reply. Most people take in what they are hearing just long enough to come up with something to say in response. They listen to comment, to advise, to diagnose, to determine a clever intervention, to direct. They are within seconds out of step and out of date with the Thinker. The Thinker knows this, and their thinking slows down. They can sense the gradual, and then accelerated, revving to speak that people do as they listen. Listening to ignite is a focus on where the Thinker will go next and on the wonder of that human mind in front of us.

How do you generate such Attention? In two words? Get interested. Get interested in the fact that the person is thinking. Keep your eyes on their eyes, breathe out and get interested. Decide that unless you have a seriously unsavoury personal emergency, you will not interrupt them. (In fact, if you could decide that today, from this point forward, you would never again interrupt people, your impact on them and the quality of your relationships would deepen immediately.)

Most of all, get interested not only in what the person is saying, but also, hugely, in what they will say *next*. When you are interested in, curious about, riveted by, what they will say next, you do not want to interrupt them.

The key feature for people of this quality of Attention is knowing they won't be interrupted. *Knowing* they won't be. Counting on it. That is what allows their mind to relax and, paradoxically, fire up. That is also what makes time to think take less time.

Knowing that we won't be interrupted is a phenomenal force for the mind. Some days it seems to me that it is just about the closest thing to heaven we can experience without dying. Some people call it magic, but it is better than magic because it is not a trick.

Consider for a moment how it might be if you and a handful of other people had been lucky enough to be invited to hear Mozart conduct and play a final draft of his 21st Piano Concerto. Let's say you are sitting there. He begins. You listen. The first movement is nearly over. Now, what you don't do is stand up suddenly and say, "Hi, uh, a quick thought here. Don't you think there are just too many notes in this thing? And also, I wonder if you could end this differently, actually better, than the way you are probably going to?"

You wouldn't do that. And it would not be because you were brought up properly and know how to behave on such an occasion. You would not interrupt because you are interested in how *Mozart* will finish the piece. You want to know what he will do next. You want *his* creation. That is why you came.

I don't think that analogy is an exaggeration. I think that the human mind in front of us as we listen is itself a generator of genius, and it is our job to be present in a particular way so that that genius can emerge. And when we are, we are more than an audience. We are a creative force for them.

Silent Incisive Questions

This whole book could be about Attention. In a way it is. Attention is implicit in all of the other nine Components. None of the others works without it. I love to learn about Attention and watch it work, to marvel at it, to notice how each experience of it deepens my respect for it.

And I love to ponder: Why does Attention with no interruption work so well? Why is it so magnificent? Why in the presence of it does the mind break through? What is going on on the inside of this Component?

Many things probably. But one I think is the presence of hundreds of silent Incisive Questions. These Incisive Questions exactly remove most core barriers to original, clear thinking – untrue limiting assumptions about the self as thinker. Our Attention is asking these silent Incisive Questions:

If you knew that you are intelligent, what thoughts would you dare to have?

If you knew that you are good, where would your thinking go next?

If you knew that you are beautiful exactly as you are, if you knew that listening to you is the most important thing I can be doing right now, if you knew that you can figure this out, that your ideas matter, that your feelings count, that you are important, that you have choice, that you can face anything, that you can solve this even when the experts haven't, that you are a delight – what new ideas would you have in this moment?

All of those questions are nested inside the interest on your face and inside the promise of no interruption, inside the warmth in your eyes, inside your interest in where they will go next, inside your trust in their intelligence.

Attention, then, seems to allow the thinker's mind to ask itself the full sequence of questions we call the Thinking Partnership Session. That sequence is the natural breakthrough process we shall examine soon. It has been right in front of us for millions of years. It is nice to see it clearly.

And so the mind in front of you, feasting on your Attention, freeing itself of the assumptions that usually silence, sings.

The Three Streams of Attention

Sometimes people think that Attention of this calibre means emptying your mind of everything and just taking in what the thinker is saying. They then apologize like mad about six months later. I cannot master this, they say, my mind keeps thinking about what the thinker has just said and however often I exorcize those thoughts, I keep having others.

How do you get your mind to be blank?

You don't. That is not only not the point; it is not even possible. You would have to be dead first. In fact, for people to think for themselves beautifully around you, you paradoxically have to keep 100 percent of your Attention in three places simultaneously:

100 percent on the *content* of what they are saying

100 percent on *your response* to what they are saying

100 percent on *the Thinking Environment* you are providing

Your mind is far from blank.

If we could make those Streams move on this page as your Attention becomes unbalanced, you would see that when one Stream begins to dominate, the others diminish. If you become fixated on the Content, you will not register your Response to it. Your face will scrunch up as you strain to understand. And the Thinking Environment will recede. You may derail the Thinker, or slow them down.

Similarly, if what they say upsets you or leads you into the couch grass of reaction and ideas that you assume to be more important than the Thinker's next thoughts, you will stop taking in the Content. And so your Response will quickly be wrong and out of date. You also will lose track of the Thinking Environment you should be creating. What you will experience almost painfully is the nearly biological urge to interrupt.

The urge to interrupt rises in proportion to the rise in the Stream of Response and the fall of the Streams of Content and Thinking Environment. But equally, if all of your Attention is on what you are doing to create a Thinking Environment, you will miss both their ideas and your response to them. You will seem artificial and detached. Which is deadly, given that one of the sources of the power of a Thinking

Environment is your steady and authentic connection to the Thinker.

Balancing the Three Streams is the secret of Attention. Blanking your mind?

Never.

Conversely, the one thing the human mind seems not able to multi-task is Attention. It can do lots of other kinds of things at the same time, but not if one of them is Attention. This is important for leaders and managers to know. But it is vital for parents to know. We cannot do other things and listen at the same time. Our children, of all ages and until the day they or we die, need us to listen to them. Listening is right up there with food and air. And love. Actually, it is love.

So, for some part of every day, when you are with your child, of any age, put away your laptop, your iPhone, your joy stick, your newspaper, your lists, your book, your wine; and turn off the TV. Be. Just be there. Be available. Your children will soon talk. Then get interested and listen. Say nothing for ages. They know when you are not listening. And it adds up. And soon, way sooner than you think, it is too late. You can't go back to their childhood and listen. They are gone.

And of all the things you can give your children, not one plasma screen, not one digital ding dong, not one pair of any kind of designer anything, not even the finest education or car or vacation can ever even touch the value of the moments you listen. They are gold. And there is no alchemy.

This goes for the grown-ups who work with you, too.

Lanz came to my office, sweating. "I have got to figure out a reply to this," he said, handing me an email. I read it. Instantly I had at least three very smart, certain-to-work, assertive things he could, should, say in his answer. The temptation was fierce to tell him what to do. Wouldn't it save time and speed things up? And after all, he had come to my office for help. But that was the point. He had come to me for *help*.

I handed the email back to him. "What do you think you should do?" I asked him.

"Don't you have any ideas?" he asked me back, addicted as most people are, to getting ideas from others, convinced through years and years of life that someone else, especially someone more senior, can think better than they can.

"Sure, I have some ideas," I said. "But you probably have better ones, and we need the best. So you tell me what you think first."

Now this email was no piece of cake to think about. In it the guy was telling Lanz that he wanted to talk about Lanz's intellectual property, Zing. I had serious doubts about whether Lanz could figure this out for himself. Intellectual property issues were not his bag. But I did my best to be still inside and to give him real Attention, to see what might happen. I was raised by an Oklahoma pioneer, and in uncharted situations like this, that gene kicks in.

"Well," he said, sitting down, "okay, my first thought is that I could get screwed here. I really need to figure out what to say to these guys if they want to make me an offer for the property. If the offer is good enough, I might want to say yes. But how will I know what good enough is?"

I absolutely knew the answer to that one. And I figured this was Lanz's biggest challenge. But I kept my Attention strong. I might be wrong, I remembered. Doubtful, but stranger things have happened. I was just barely holding onto the principle that the brain that generates the question usually generates the best answer.

"And will they have any regard for my interest in this? Forget it," he went on, proving me right about being wrong. "They will hope I don't know a whole lot about intellectual property and can make their own wild profit on it.

"So, I need to think about what to say based on what they offer. So, if they offer…"

Lanz stopped. I had so many ideas for him I was exhausted bopping them all on the head. But he did not beg me for them, and so I kept quiet and continued to be interested in what he would say next.

He looked at me. He had that face of someone both far away and up too close to see.

"Nope," he said with a snap, "that's not it. That's not even remotely it. I don't need to figure out what they might say and how I will respond. I need to figure out *what I want* and propose that first. I need to take charge of this thing! Who is running this show anyway? It is my IP, and I can start by thinking about what I really want to do with Zing long term, whether I actually do want to sell the rights to it in the first place."

I smiled. He smiled. "Well," he said, "what do you know? Never thought I'd end up here. I feel great. And I want to go off and figure out now what I do want with these guys. No, correction, what I do want to do with *Zing*. What I really *want*. Hey, thanks. That was amazing. Thanks for the ideas."

And he left. From reactive to proactive, victim to in-charge in under five minutes. I had said nothing. Not one idea had come from me and yet he gave me all the credit. My Attention had done it. I shook my head at the thought of how much longer it would have taken if I had succumbed to my urge to insert my ideas and be the expert. Days? Certainly hours. And what a boring mess it would have been. More important, I wonder whether he would ever have gotten to the proactive perspective at all. I shuddered.

This kind of Attention begins with respect. It begins, as Bill said, with love. Love is not usually the way we describe the essence of professional relationships. But surely if love is anything, it is unfettered respect for things wondrous and fecund, things like the human mind and the human life it expresses. Love is what makes Attention catalytic.

It is love of the person's mind. Love of their capability. Love of their yet un-thought thoughts that only they, not you, can generate, but that your Attention makes possible. It is love of their goodness. Love, most of all, of their intelligence. And it is love like this, beamed through your Attention, that is the change-maker, the fire on the tip of the finger.

And if we don't love? If we confuse helping with doing for and having the answers; if we crave more to direct with our questions and impress with our tools; if we see ourselves as the experts because of what we say, not because of how we are, with people, what is lost?

It is the person that is lost. It is the best answers that are lost. It is the perfect way forward that is lost. Sometimes even the possibilities are lost. Words struggle to point clearly enough to the size of this disappearance. It is not much less than the snuffing of life.

So, you agree to love people – to respect them as thinking beings – with all your heart; and you know as you do this that you will have the privilege of listening to what matters most to them, to what they really do think, to the truth as they discover it. You will have the privilege of helping a human being find the way, crystallize, take responsibility and soar safely.

Listening this way, focusing and letting go all at once, letting reverence mix with scrutiny, holding dear the source – the human mind in front of you – is to raise your arms and twirl in the sun, to be permeated with that unique purpose that is human connection at its finest.

Attention for each other, Attention at this level, is, I think, the key missing piece in our world. Once we can give Attention like this, once we understand its generative impact on human thinking, we will, I believe, re-think more things even than our own challenging life dilemmas. We may even think anew about whole structures of work and economics and global relationships. We may then grow intelligent interdependence and wave goodbye forever to destructive competition and the ravaging of one group to feed the addicts of the other.

I think until we practise and understand this kind of Attention, we might as well just drink beer on porches all day and stop rushing around pretending we are progressing human society.

Look at our world. Walk around it. Can you see the need? Can you see how simple it could be to fill it? Can you then moan into the morning, to see how we, most intelligent of all sentient beings, just don't do it?

We will do well to go back to Bill's words, uttered on the threshold of life's biggest mystery of all. "When we love him, we get to listen. And then, we get to listen more and more."

Our world is crying out for this simple thing: Attention to free the human mind to think for itself, afresh.

It is this.

It is definitely, so definitely, this.

CHAPTER 4

Do We Believe In It?

Equality

Regarding each other as thinking peers

Giving equal turns and Attention

Honouring boundaries

Even in a hierarchy people can be equal as thinkers

Knowing you will have your turn improves the quality of your Attention

Do we really believe in Equality? I mean really, as in cross our hearts?

Equality shows up in just about every list of Core Values. Of course we believe in it.

But Equality as thinkers? Do we mean that? I mean, have you ever actually stopped yourself on the way to a meeting and thought, now, as I go into this meeting, do I believe in Equality? Are we *all* thinking equals here?

And certainly if you were to stop people in the hall and say, "Hi, quick question – do you believe in Equality? I mean, really believe in it? Just curious." And smiled. How weird would that look? Actually, stopping anyone these days on the way to anything, even the bathroom, is seriously career-limiting. So give up that idea.

But wouldn't it be good if every six months or so that question were on every meeting agenda, and everyone was expected to answer it? And then expected to face its implications?

The fact is there are a lot of naked emperors bouncing off the walls of our organizations. And "Do we really believe in Equality?" would make them at least get dressed.

Once dressed they would have to face the ravages of inequality – the silent siphoning of quality from decisions. And that is serious. When a few people do the thinking, most people do not. When most people do not, most perspectives, most insights, most fresh ideas, most analyses, most inspiration, most shinings of the light never happen.

Too many of our decisions are stupid. And so much of what the world needs it doesn't get. All of this on purpose. All of this because actually, darling, we don't believe in Equality. Not really.

Let's equate the human mind with a state-of-the-art machine. Cost? A billion dollars each. Each has two switches, T and F. T for Tiny capacity; F for Full capacity. We have bought ten of these things. But let's switch only three of them to Full. Let's keep the other seven at Tiny. Let's waste seven billion dollars every day. How about it?

This makes the nut in the hall asking the Equality question look pretty sane.

But, let's say you say, okay, we need everyone's thinking. Let's say you agree that we need access to the fullest and best ideas in order to make the best decisions and build the best organization and a world that works truly well for truly everyone. Let's just say we need all human minds on Full. How then do we do it, you ask? Because, believe me, you say, a lot of these people can't seem to string two intelligent ideas together even when I ask them to; and when I call on them there is not exactly an explosion of genius.

Absolutely.

But you just need to do a couple of things differently.

First, you need to *regard* them as your equal. Really, as in cross your heart and hope to die. Then you need to *show* them.

One to one you do this by wanting to know what they think, then by asking them what they think, then by giving them equal *time* to express what they think, then by listening with generative Attention as described in Chapter 3, then by asking them (in some way that doesn't sound like you just read Chapter 3) what more they think.

That's all. *Regard* them as your thinking equal. And *show* them.

As professionals we have the hardest time with this. As helpers, advisors, carers, psychologists, lawyers, doctors, teachers, coaches we are taught that we think better than our clients. By definition. And that we have the answers. By definition. That is what people pay us for.

The idea that our clients or patients or students are equal to us as thinkers and should have at least equal time to think and speak seems absurd. What is the point of the professional if the client can think as well as (or even better than) the professional can?

Professionals have two points. The first is to be a Thinking Environment for the client so that they can think for themselves brilliantly and discover the best way forward. The second is to offer information and experience and insight to the client that may be of value. But that should be about 20 percent of the interaction. Because when people go to professionals, what they are looking for first and most of all is a person who wants to know what they think, who they are and what matters to them. Only after all of that do they want to be told what to do. They don't articulate this, nor sometimes even know it consciously, but they want it. They say so when interviewed. And when deciding to change professionals.

Between professionals and their staff this Equality needs to prevail, too. The cost of inequality is too high.

A surgeon, standing scrubbed with both gloved hands in the air, called for the scalpel. The faceless attendant handed it to him. The doctor settled the scalpel just over the left upper abdomen. The voice of the attendant next to him squeaked, then spoke, "Dr Janes, forgive me, but that is the wrong side." The doctor suspended his hand an inch over the body. He turned his head to find the head of the voice. He froze his eyes on the voice's eyes.

"What did you say?" The attendant took the breath that precedes words. Before the words came, the doctor shouted, "I know what you said. And I caution you, don't ever, ever do that again."

The attendant's hands began to shake. "But sir, it is the right kidney that is damaged."

"I warn you, Ms Reynolds, you are out of line."

The doctor cut into the left side. He removed the left kidney. He ordered the patient sewn up. He returned to his rounds. The next day he was summoned to the hospital chief executive's office and dismissed. Six months later his medical licence was withdrawn. He had removed the healthy kidney.

Now that was expensive. And at fault there was the assumption of inequality. Made deadly by arrogance. Not an unusual combination.

Similarly, the still-worst accidental airline crash in history, Tenerife, 1977, seems almost certainly to have been caused by the pilot's rejection of Equality in the cockpit. Two jumbo jets had emergency-landed on Tenerife, having been diverted because of socked-in impossible landing conditions on Majorca. One of the jets was trying to cross one runway, unable to see through the increasing fog there.

The other jet was at the end of that runway, the pilot angry and impatient to get into the air before the fog worsened. He started his engines and began to taxi. The flight engineer shouted, "You can't go. We don't have clearance." The pilot slammed on the brake and screamed at the engineer, "I make the decisions here. I will do what I think is best. Is that understood?"

A few minutes later the pilot started again. Again the flight engineer shouted to him to stop. But this time the pilot accelerated at full speed. He could not see that the other jumbo jet was still trying to cross the runway. Seconds later he saw the plane, could not stop his own, and so pulled up on the stick praying to lift far enough above the other plane to clear it. But he cut right through the body of the other plane, killing 583 people.

Again the divesting of Equality and the donning of arrogance. Again a deadly combination.

In groups, too, people arrive wanting, and able, to think. And in groups people need you as the leader to regard them as their thinking equal, and then show them. Inside a dependable meeting structure of Equality, they will almost certainly think well, sometimes brilliantly (Chapter 48 shows you step by step how to do this.) And you will save those seven billion dollars every day.

How powerful can that be? Go back to Martin Kalungu-Banda. Recall Martin's first message to the new Zambian President, "Serve, Mr President." And remember the President's willingness to learn from Martin, a person not even in the hierarchy, much less at the top of it; and then deciding to take in Martin's thinking even as it stood in stark opposition to his own; and then to offer to the diplomats an assumption and a structure of Equality. Look what happened. A country's revenue salvaged. Lives saved. Esteem preserved. Joy ignited. Not bad for 36 minutes and the decision to embrace the uncomplicated concept of Equality.

I think it is worth considering that a professional's first job, a leader's first job, a parent's first job is to create the conditions for people to think for themselves, saturating it with Equality.

Respecting Boundaries

Equality in a Thinking Environment has two definitions. The first we have just explored: regarding each other as thinking Equals. The second is respecting Boundaries.

Boundaries protect our equality as thinkers.

I need to know that you do not expect my thinking to be your thinking. If I know that, I can think for myself and add quality to your thinking, and you to mine. We may not agree. Or we may. But even inside agreement my thinking will be mine; and yours, yours.

To think well, I also need to know that you do not expect my turn to be your turn. First, I need to know absolutely that you will not interrupt me. Then I need to know that you are interested in what I think, not formulating your turn in your head, pacing until I finish.

To think well I also need to know that you do not need my victory to be your victory.

Boundaries are possibly the most important invisible thing in our lives. All of the other invisible things depend on it. Love, most of all. And respect, admiration, happiness, independence, interdependence. Boundaries are not barriers. They do not keep us apart. They, in fact, bring us together. If I know you are not trying to be me or trying to get me to be you, I can be truly *with* you. I can give up protecting myself from you. I can, thereby, stop focusing on myself and become more giving, more *with* you.

To be safe in who we are lets us be fully with another person.

Boundaries protect us. And so we trust. And so we can relax. And suddenly we realize we can grow close. And we can keep thinking.

"Nancy, I want you to sit way across this room, over there." One of my earliest clients was telling me what would work best for him in our time together. "And I want you not to say a single word, not one, for as long as it takes me to think this issue through, and that might be quite a while. I might cry, but I might not, and I don't want you to care about that. The main thing is, don't speak."

I think it was at that moment that I first really understood about boundaries. I had been studying peer counselling, and in that process there was a certain amount of directing of the client to their feelings, or to a point of view chosen by the counsellor.

This client was I think making sure I did not do any of that. And he had a hugely productive session.

It turned that part of my definition of "professional" upside down. I spent months trying to figure out what happened there.

Boundaries are a way of being with each other as equals so that each of us stands in the light.

Boundaries are also probably one reason why Equality in meetings in a Thinking Environment works so beautifully. If I am chairing, I agree to see you as a person separate from me. I do not require you to be like or agree with me. I define loyalty as your doing your finest thinking for the good of the organization, not as your pleasing me. I do not look to you for sameness. I look to you for authenticity. Equality depends on this.

We began this exploration of Equality with the question: do we believe in it? But perhaps we should instead be asking: Is it generally warranted? Is it true that one person thinks as well as another? Not just, do we believe we are equal as thinkers? But *are* we?

We can answer that question by setting up Thinking Environments and observing results. And so far the results are impressive. We seem to get functionally smarter when Equality is present. Everyone does. And when we know we can trust Equality not to deteriorate, we get smarter still.

And that is enough for me. If people begin to think coherently or creatively at unprecedented new levels because I treat them as my thinking equal, I don't really care what their background, training, IQ, SAT score, degree or university was.

I care that they are now thinking, better and better. And I care that the groups they are serving are served better because they are treating them as equals, too.

I care that the human mind finally comes out for a jog, breathes deeply, sees what is real and lets that tiny dapple of sun lead the way. I care that the world flourishes as a result. Equality helps make that happen.

And I think that, like President Mwanawasa, we must have the courage to trust it.

CHAPTER 5

What Is Your Hurry?

Ease

Offering freedom from internal rush or urgency

Ease creates; urgency destroys

When it comes to helping people think for themselves, sometimes doing means not doing

Isadora Duncan danced with scarves. They emerged from her fingers. Her tunic-ed body seemed to issue them to canopy and permeate her movement. She described the dancer as "speaking in movement out of the self, and out of something greater than all selves." Audiences in the 1920s were outraged – and riveted. They woke the next day, re-garbing in wool and seams, top to toe. But they recalled the scarves and the tiny tunic and the waving, willowy, watery soul that was her dance. Working in their wool, they remembered.

I often think of Isadora's dance when I watch Attention work. To be its best, Attention, from inside itself it seems, summons Ease. Ease emerges and sweeps and dips and saunters, draping itself around Attention's focus, allowing it dimensions greater than focus alone can produce.

This all happens inside. Not outside. Sure, it would be wonderful if we could stop the everyday madness around us, the squeezing and lunging and accelerating that pass for normal at work these days. But this external state shows no signs of letting up. That will probably not happen until Ease takes over our internal selves first.

So Ease in a Thinking Environment is an inside thing. You slow down. You still your internal day. You focus. You notice that you exist and that you are in this very moment and in this very room and with this very person. You see them. You let yourself let them be. You say how long you have. You keep that boundary clear so that you can be fully there with them, letting distractions deflate. You will get to the ravenous Blackberry right after this. This human in front of you is more important.

But surely Ease will take too long. Surely problems cannot be solved without fear and tension and the fist-pounding panicking proctors of our production line of overnight outcomes. Surely we should hurry up. Surely if we stop and ask people what they think, and then listen, at ease inside, we will burn, and by dawn the winds will take out the whole valley. Surely I did not just witness Ease enrich Attention, and Attention unleash the human mind. Did I? Anyway, outrageous to wear nothing but a tunic and scarves. Not even shoes. Surely....

No, actually. Isadora was right. And there are many dances. One speaks about the power of Ease in generating independent, excellent human thinking, too. Why, then, do we see Ease work its wonders on the human mind, but return to hurry in such a hurry?

What is it about 120 steps a minute and tight jaws and pounding hearts that drag us back in such a flash? Why can't we see how brilliant Ease is in birthing brilliance? Why can't we see that brilliance from each person is the point of our work because everything depends on it, and that rush kills it dead, and that because of rush and the death of thinking, the world, not just the valley, is in flames?

We bought an equation, that's why. Rushed = Important. Tense = Focused. Tight = Professional. Pressured = Alive. They are all the same thing. And not one is true. But they infest our way of being with each other. Not every culture is un-easeful, of course. But where are those cultures in the collective league table lore of successful, leading, take-them-seriously cultures of the world? They are right at the top of the "not-yet-developed" world. They make it to "developed" as soon as they begin to tighten up, build pressure, forego naps, walk fast and assiduously scoop up more. "Developed" countries are the ones that have been doing that for ages – and are terrified of scarves.

The true equation, not for sale when we were buying, is: Ease = Quality. Try it. Be with someone today. Ask them what they think about something and decide that for up to ten minutes (you are not going to die or go broke in ten minutes) you are going to be interested in what they will say next, that you will breathe out, stop picking at the skin around your thumb nail, keep your eyes on their eyes (or whatever your culture does with eyes to demonstrate Attention), and that if they stop thinking and are looking to you for the answers, you are going to ask them what more they think.

Breathe out again, smile a little, pull your eyeballs off the screen or the ceiling or the pencil you are threatening with a broken back. Just be with this person. Take them in. Notice them. They are thinking. And the more at ease you are inside as they do, the better they do it.

But I am a fire fighter, you say, rushing is crucial. No. Even fire fighters fight fires better, they tell me, if they are at ease *inside*, so they can think! So they can listen to each other and to the thousands of bits of information speaking to them from the scene.

Ease inside allows us to think about the emergencies outside.

And never mind fires. Even our tense conversations feel like emergencies. When Ease disappears from these conversations, usually right at the beginning, thinking stops.

Erin decided to outwit this habit between her and Tod. Periodically, she seemed to anger him. His anger was not fierce, but it shook her up. She hated conflict, so shaking her up wasn't hard. Usually when he told her what was making him angry, she collapsed into the assumption that she was bad, stupid, unlovable and irredeemable. And that led her to scour her mind for evidence that Tod's points were invalid. She then interrupted. That made him more angry. And that made her more desperate. No one was thinking.

She decided that the next time he needed to tell her he was angry, she would ask herself this question over and over as he spoke: If I knew I am good and lovable and intelligent even when Tod is angry, how would I be inside as he speaks? Ease summed it up. So she determined to hold onto Ease through every word he spoke. This felt like a NASA launch, but she was committed.

And it worked. He said he was angry. She said, "I would love to know what is upsetting you." And she kept her Attention on him the whole time. She decided and re-decided by the second to be objectively interested in what he was feeling and in the annoyances he was recounting. She recited in her head the Incisive Question when she was losing traction, and that brought her back to Ease, and that brought her back to interest, and that brought her back to thinking.

She asked him if there was more he wanted to say. She asked that in different ways three times before he was truly finished. Then she had a short turn, agreed with the things she agreed with, and offered a different point of view of the other things; and they agreed that all was now well, and it was over. Ease had prevailed. She was proud of herself. But most of all she was impressed by how much simpler that was. Easy, no. Uncomplicated, yes. And better.

Ease works like that. Easily. Storms may rage outside. But inside we can be still. And with our Attention the person thinking in front of us will, almost suddenly, begin to think well. Better than we could have for them.

But strangely, after experiencing Ease from us, they do not automatically do it for others. It is as if they don't see what is happening. It is right in front of them, but they don't recognize it. They don't inquire about it, take it apart, understand it. They love it, but without instruction they don't learn it.

So about 25 years ago I decided to teach it, to make Ease conscious, to offer it to people as a skill, a competency, like skydiving or SWAT analysis or folding linen.

I am glad I did, because teaching it works. People can learn how to generate Ease, particularly when they see first hand, often dramatically, how much better people think around them as a result. People want to be around Ease.

So, yes, after experiencing it, they step back into their wools: interrupting, criticizing, tensing, overtaking in order, they think, to get ahead.

But they want to learn Ease. Somewhere they remember the scarves. Somewhere they do remember.

CHAPTER 6

Why Praise Praise?

Appreciation

Practising a 5:1 ratio of appreciation to criticism

The human mind thinks more rigorously and creatively in a context of genuine appreciation

It turns out humans need Appreciation. Biologically, I mean. To function well. People can no longer call Appreciation an indulgence. Well, they can. But now they will be embarrassingly behind the times. Biology has spoken. And isn't it just so nice when the hard physical research proves what has been softly observable all along? I love those days.

Here's what one research team found: Using a neuro-imaging technique called the SPECT scan, Drs Noelle Nelson, Daniel Amen and Jeannine Lemare Calaba studied how appreciative thoughts and feelings affected blood flow to the brain. They found that less blood flows to the brain, particularly to the cerebellum, cingulated gyrus and the left basal ganglia when we are thinking critical thoughts. Blood flows to those areas well, on the other hand, when we are thinking appreciative thoughts. Appreciation, it seems, is necessary for optimal brain functioning. Thinking needs blood, and blood needs Appreciation. Lovely.

And there is another bit of biological news: When the heart's rhythm and pattern are at healthy levels, the cortex gets active. And, get this: in the presence of Appreciation the rhythm and pattern of the heart move toward those healthy levels. So Appreciation moves through the heart (and its 40,000 neurons) to stimulate the brain to work better. Once again, Appreciation improves thinking. Very nice.

I learned this from Lloyd Chapman and Helena Dolny who taught me about the research work of The HeartMath Research Center in

California. Lloyd said, "I am interested in the Ten Components of a Thinking Environment in light of this research on the heart and cortex." I assumed he meant the one Component of Appreciation. Kind of like un-factoring a quadratic equation.

But he didn't. He meant all of The Ten Components. I was ages getting this. (Untrue assumptions slow you down.) But when I did, I was jumping. *Each* Component is an act of Appreciation. And all ten in place at once is a *system* of Appreciation. The whole Thinking Environment stimulates the heart to establish a healthy rhythm and pattern, which then stimulates the brain. Ah.

He said other interesting things, too, such as how executives can now stop buying the tiny cool biofeedback machines that help them stabilize their hearts in times of high stress (all day) in order to stimulate their cortices. (Apparently executives need to think better.) He said that Appreciation is doing the job instead. Appreciation stabilizes the heart and stimulates thinking. (Appreciation is cheaper, but it is harder, apparently, for the executives to master. Still, they persevere. Recessions have some benefits.)

This research and I could not agree more. Demonstrably, people do think better in the presence of Appreciation. And they stop thinking in the presence of criticism. So much for the insatiable need of managers and teachers and parents and pastors to flagellate us with our faults. It just does not work. It never has.

What works is to see our strengths; to look objectively at what we are doing well and to build on that; to see what is good and say it, to others and ourselves. When we thoroughly know how good we are, we can readily (and creatively) *think* well about how to improve. It is as simple as that.

Observing this effect of Appreciation on thinking, we included it in the list of the Ten Components from the outset. And following the research of John and Julie Gottman, referred to in *Time To Think*, page 66, we set the ratio of Appreciation to criticism at 5:1.

So, in the face of all this, what will happen to the world's worship of criticism, and its executive version, cynicism? Slow death, I predict. Death because criticism does not produce good thinking. Slow, because Appreciation is terrifying. Strong word, I know, but people struggle with Appreciation. To give it or to receive it. They love it. But they hate it more. That is, they think they should hate it. They have absorbed the lore that Appreciation is not the road to acuity; that you can't trust it; that it is cheesy; that it is just "not done". For all of these read: terrifying.

One day opened my eyes to this fear. Mohammed's executive team invited me to deliver a special follow-up day to the Transforming Meetings programme. "We need you to make us appreciate each other," he said.

Make them? Grown up, powerful men in suits?

"We value it. It helps us think," his colleague said. "But we just can't do it."

Can't? I looked around at these economists who could do things with numbers and theories and graphs that most of us on the planet don't even know the words for.

And I thought, "In light of the research, this translates to: we have been cultured away from the capacity to do the very thing that helps human beings think, and thus live and perform, at their best."

So I "made" the economists appreciate each other. They identified a quality they had come to respect in each of their colleagues. They wrote it down. Then in turn, with everyone else listening, they said it.

The man being appreciated had to listen, too, without saying, "humph", and without looking away or squirming (lots of knees going up and down under the table notwithstanding).

Then when the Appreciation was complete, the man appreciated had to say, simply, "thank you". Not to say, "thank you" is effectively to trash the person's thinking. Even when the thinking just happens to be positive things about you.

Having been sufficiently shocked by this team's love-hate relationship with Appreciation, I found myself becoming jaded about this Component in corporate life. But, life, loathing lethargy, knocked me the other direction just as dramatically one day.

A leading airline had adopted the Thinking Environment as their management culture. They invited me to chair a meeting, so that they could see it done "right". I agreed. I had a wonderful time touring the building ahead of the meeting (except for the moment when the Head of HR opened the door to the flight control centre, and everyone's eyes came off their screens. All those little dots disappearing in that second swept through my imagination, and I rushed out.)

The meeting was excellent. All Thinking Environment processes worked. We had five minutes left. Perfect. Just enough for a Closing Round to reflect on the success of the meeting. Not enough time, I conjectured, to appreciate each other. And, anyway, executives can't do that, right?

I said, "So, to end, shall we have a Round to say what we think went well in the meeting?" A hush. They looked at each other. "Don't they do a Closing Success Round about the meeting?" I wondered. "Is this going to be the first Thinking Environment feature they have failed to incorporate into their practice?"

More hush. Then the Director said, "With all due respect, Nancy, we always close with Appreciation for each other as well." Always? Well, well.

Can't and always. You just never know.

Appreciation keeps us thinking well. But at this very moment billions of people are not doing it. They want to. But they aren't. They are just sitting there with each other not doing it. Why?

Mandy figured this out for herself.

"What more do you want to achieve in this session?" I asked her.

"I want to appreciate my parents."

Moving on to what she needed next in order to keep thinking for herself (much more on this sequence of questions soon), I asked, "What are you assuming that stops you from appreciating your parents?"

"I am assuming they won't receive it; that they will dismiss it. I am assuming that my appreciation skills are poor."

"What else are you assuming that stops you from appreciating your parents?" I asked.

"That I might not get it right; that they have got to appreciate me before I show them Appreciation. That they will dismiss it. That's all."

"And of those assumptions, which is the one most stopping you from appreciating your parents?"

Mandy thought about that for nearly a minute. Then she said, "I am assuming that they have to receive it in order for me to give it."

Very energetic suddenly, she said, "And that is not true! My need is to appreciate them, not to be appreciated for appreciating them!"

Sharing her excitement, I asked, "So, if it is not true that they have to receive it in order for you to give it, what are your words for what is true and liberating?"

"What is true and liberating is that what I give is entirely up to me."

Then, constructing the Incisive Question in *her* words, I asked her, "If you knew that what you give is entirely up to you, how would you appreciate your parents?"

Her eyes sparkled. "From now on, I would preface our conversations with appreciation of them."

Giving her the chance to generate more ideas, I asked her again, "If you knew that what you give is entirely up to you, how else would you appreciate your parents?"

"I would reminisce with them about my childhood, highlighting things they did that I am grateful for. And I would tell them I love them."

She cried a little and wrote down the question. She smiled. "Thank you," she said. "I just wish I had realized this 20 years ago. Appreciation is so easy. But it is so hard. It's because of the untrue assumptions, isn't it?"

Yes, and maybe there is nothing more important than finding those assumptions and replacing them. And then appreciating everyone in our lives from morning to night.

And as we do, we can remember three S's. Not to veer into a gimmick here, but these three things seem to help us receive and give Appreciation:

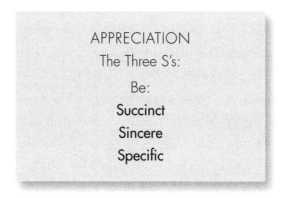

APPRECIATION
The Three S's:
Be:
Succinct
Sincere
Specific

Be succinct because people cannot hear very much Appreciation. They fall down a rabbit hole of disbelief. You know this because they begin to sweat.

Be sincere because that disbelief is just waiting to pounce on your words anyway, and because getting lies is worse than getting no Appreciation.

Be specific because, oddly, the more specific you are, the more a person can apply the Appreciation generally to their lives.

Mohammed was right. Even if the idea sounds too "just not done" at first, actually everyone longs to receive and give appreciation.

Teenagers love it, too. At our school every student had a day when everyone else in their group of 25 appreciated them. We called it "The Birthday Circle", whether it was their birthday or not.

Jim Perkey loved this idea. He invited his group of 20 campers to have an Appreciation Circle to mark the end of camp. One person sat in the middle of the group, and everyone else said what they valued and would miss about that person. Jim had allocated the hour before lunch for this. They started.

They were articulate. They were sincere. They did not rush. And after only six people, they had to run to lunch, thirty minutes late. The campers then asked if they could take their 90 minutes of "free time" in the afternoon to finish the Circle. And two hours into that, still not finished, they missed supper and had to ask the cooks for something from the kitchen. They then got special permission to meet after the last campfire. That meant they resumed the Circle at midnight. At 3am they finished. They lingered, even longer, reluctant to go.

Six hours total. 20 teenagers appreciating each other. One minute per appreciation. Worth all of the time in the world. And its effect lasting most likely a lifetime.

Appreciation from the outside sets up liberating assumptions and Incisive Questions on the inside. When we tell each other what we value in each other, for example, it is as if we ask the question, "If you knew that you are good, what would you think or feel or do?"

Silent Incisive Questions are probably the reason why explicit Appreciation frees thinking. And with all that blood flowing so nicely to the brain and the cortex being stimulated by a smiling heart, who can be surprised?

Remember also, there are inexplicit ways to appreciate people, too. Asking people the question, "What do you think?" and then giving them Attention without interruption is a powerful way to appreciate them. As is listening to them beautifully about anything anytime. As is smiling when they walk into the room. As is being at ease, however rough the seas.

Maybe it goes like this:

When we appreciate each other, we think better.

When we think better, we love better.

When we love better, we live better.

And that is the point of it all, anyway. Isn't it?

CHAPTER 7

How Brave Are You?

Encouragement

Building courage to go to the unexplored edge of ideas by eliminating competition between thinkers

To be "better than" is not necessarily to be good

I must be more. Most of all, I must be more than you. Smarter than you. Richer than you. Trendier than you. More successful than you. More influential than you. More anything than you.

More.

So sums up one of the dumbest, but most persuasive, assumptions ever to pitch camp in the collective human psyche. More, more, more. Better, better, better.

Let's start over. What would change in our world if we just stopped all this competition once and for all, and started championing instead? The first thing is that thinking would improve. Competition is not good for thinking, certainly not for original, desperately-needed-by-the-world thinking.

Of course, better-than is not all bad. Some things *are* better than other things. And striving to be better is sometimes important. But, as we explored in *Time To Think*, being better-than does not necessarily mean being good in the first place. It means merely that we are better than whatever the first place was. And that could be – often is in fact – not particularly good at all.

Being better-than, competing-with, is so taken for granted as a good thing that it is gushing through our global bloodstream. In fact, we carry a cross for competition. We worship it. And, not to go toofar with this analogy, we then crucify each other on it. More specifically, we crucify each other's courageous thinking.

Courageous thinking needs freedom from preoccupation with what others are thinking of our thinking. It needs trust. It needs Ease. And so it rarely takes place in life's Petri dish of competition. Encouragement in a Thinking Environment is the *building of courage to go to the unexplored edge of ideas by eliminating competition between thinkers.*

This is crucial in leadership teams.

Now, you wouldn't think that teams, given the definition of "team" (co-operative body working *together* toward a common goal, etc) would go in for competition with each other. But there you would be wrong. Teams leave the Petri dish in the dust. (Some ideas are so outrageous, they require a mixed metaphor.)

In fact, some team leaders think that competition among the members of the team is essential for high performance. Actually, all it is essential for is mercurial self-esteem and misdirected caution. When you focus on what others are thinking of what you are thinking, you aren't thinking. Not very well. You are running a second-by-second gauntlet of calculation about how you are doing in everyone's eyes, especially the leaders'.

Consider these two approaches to building team culture:

Executive 1

Definitely, I promote competition between the team members. I think it makes everyone work harder and aspire to more. I might say something like, John, your idea is crap. Saul's idea was damn good. How can you improve on yours? Or, let's hear from everyone on this. I will be listening for the sharpest, best idea. We will go with that one, and whoever thought of it will get dinner on me.

Our meetings are very lively. Very energetic. We don't waste time listening past any lame point in someone's idea.

The person who can spot the weakness in the argument or the inaccuracy in the data is expected to jump in and take over immediately, steer the discussion some place better. So people's focus during the discussions is very sharp, looking for the holes and for bad reasoning.

Also, we have "Best Idea of the Month" contests.

And we post the percentage of new client acquisition growth so people can see who is ahead.

"Which guy can you leave in the dust today?" I like to ask. Great question. It works. People in my team work their butts off. We should probably make that question into a poster.

Executive 2

I used to think competition was good wherever and whenever. But I discovered two years ago that there's competition and then there's competition. The first is okay. The second is a killer. In fact, the second kills the first.

The first drives you to improve your own performance and to make a better mousetrap. (But I sometimes wonder how the world would be different if humans had put ingenuity into keeping mice out of the house in the first place, rather than killing them once they got in.)

Anyway, the trouble starts with the second kind, the minute people start thinking together, but start competing instead. When we compete, we cling to safe ground because we are trying to be smarter-than or to look-better-than or to win-more-praise-than. Then we don't listen long enough. We don't venture adventurous solutions. And that usually means regurgitating and reshaping the familiar. It usually means just painting brighter the stripe down the known way.

So, I discourage competition among team members. I require and reward what I call "The Adventurer Priest", the practice of listening hard and generously because you want to know what the person really thinks, and because you want cutting-edge, discovery thinking more than you want to be the one to come up with it.

And then when it is your turn, you move out past your desire to be seen to be smarter than the others, or to be loyal. You move to the hard questions, the upheaval-ing questions, and then to good ideas.

My teams are thinking better now. They have more courage. And they have more energy. They also say they look forward to the meetings.

It won't surprise you that I vote for Executive 2. I would kill myself before I worked for Executive 1. I won't elaborate. I will simply encourage you to give courage as Executive 2 did.

And I am not kidding about the courage, because the truth about the effect of competition on thinking lies deep in the unspoken experience of competition's sophisticated victims – our executives, our managers, our entrepreneurs, our leaders. They swear by it. As I said, they worship it. But when they fall into bed at night, somewhere where the truth whispers to them, they know that they are dying from it.

But they can't question, can they, the road of reward, even when the signs are faces with toothy grins? Who can stop in the middle and question? Who can strike out across the field?

Maybe you can. Everything truly good in our world has begun with the people who did.

And by the way, Executive 2's point about physical energy was right. As Bill Ford (author of *High Energy Habits*, Simon & Schuster) says, physical energy comes from many things besides exercise or food; one of them is from the freedom to be yourself without trying to be better-than, and from the experience of being championed.

And from that comes independent thinking.

And from that comes the results-rich impact of Encouragement.

CHAPTER 8

What Are You Not Facing?

Information

Supplying the facts

Dismantling denial

Withholding or denying information results in intellectual vandalism

Facing what you have been denying frees you to think clearly

We think of information as facts – what time the train leaves, how many microbes live in a dishcloth, how rooks know where to put the first twig for the nest, whether the budget allows for a balloon ride.

Whatever the issue, accurate information is crucial to thinking well about it. You could argue that until you have full and accurate information about something, you shouldn't even bother to think about it. So, facts, figures, data – all of that matters when it comes to thinking well. (That is why I think that withholding information is an act of intellectual vandalism.)

In a Thinking Environment we also define information as the *dismantling of denial*. This is much more interesting. Denial is the assumption that what is true is not true. Or conversely, that what is not true, is. People live in some kind of denial a shocking amount of the time.

Individual denial is bad enough: He's not drunk; he is just exhausted every single night and so slurs a lot; Making this one purchase on our only not-maxed-out card won't matter; I am lying, but she will never find out; Yes, he hit me, but he is not a violent person; My trousers are tight – they shrank. Individual denial. Terrible for you. Terrible for your relationships.

But even more terrible is organizational denial, mostly because it savages lives. Organizational denial can keep corruption and autocratic leadership in place. And it is a bear to dismantle.

The Three Stages Of Denial

There seem to be three stages of organizational denial to watch out for. This is how they played out in one team meeting:

Jane's team was in a discussion. In the middle of Rachel's sentence Jane savaged her. Jane said, "Rachel, is it possible you are an idiot? You question every damn thing." Jane's attack escalated in volume and in tone and denigration. It ended with, "I don't know why we ever hired you in the first place."

That was bad. But what was amazing was that no one stopped her. Each person sat there, frozen, allowing it to go on and on and on. Abuse was occurring in front of everyone, but no one moved; and most important, no one could think.

When it was over, as if nothing had happened (keep that phrase in mind), Jane turned back to the agenda. Everyone, subdued and cautious, nevertheless continued with the agenda, too.

That is Denial Stage One: *What is happening is not happening.*

Afterwards when two of the team members met over the Flavia machine, Lucy said, "Well, I guess that proves it: no one messes with Jane. How brutal was that scene?"

"Yeah, but that's just Jane's style, Sam said. "Especially when she is under pressure. And Rachel's questions are a pain sometimes. Anyway, it wasn't so bad. Nobody died."

"True."

That was Denial Stage Two: *It happened, but it was not bad.*

And a few minutes later a colleague from another team came over to them and said, "Wow, I hear that was some meeting you guys just had."

Sam said, "Well, not really. It was pretty good in the end."

Lucy said, "And the best thing was that we got right through that wicked agenda."

That was Denial Stage Three: *The bad was good.*

Denial often works in this way: three stages in which people quickly re-construct reality and then offer as true what was never true in the first place.

Meeting after meeting this denial kept both the team and outsiders from challenging Jane about her behaviour, and thus prevented its being stopped. And those three stages of denial sabotaged good thinking in that team for months afterward.

The injunction from the lips of denial is:

> Ignore this.
> Then distort it.
> Then rewrite it.

It is a sinister cycle.

But certain questions dismantle denial and restore accurate information. Four effective ones (asked with Ease and with Attention) are:

> What you are not facing that is right in front of your face?
>
> What are you assuming that lets you ignore this?
>
> If you were to face it, what positive outcomes might result?
>
> If you knew that you can handle the fall out, what steps would you take to live free of this denial?

We deny not only the bad things. We deny the good things, too. Usually this is Information about ourselves. In fact, the chances are good that right now you are denying lots of good things about yourself. And that is as dangerous as denying the bad things.

Florence was intelligent. People loved her – her wit, her incisive grasp of the issues, her warmth, her energy. They loved her most when she was most herself, full-out, as she called it.

But a lot of the time she held back. And sometimes she held back in exactly the situations in which people most wanted her to be full out. She stayed in her office just when they wanted her in the company's other locations. She read from a script just when she should be speaking from her heart. She stopped exercising just when she had gotten her body to a place that pleased her.

"I am assuming that full-out is dangerous," she told me. "I am assuming that people will criticize me if I look too good or risk saying what I really think; if I am too energetic, they will say I am too much. If I am fully me; they won't like it."

"Do you think it is it true," I asked her, "that if you are fully you, they won't like it?"

Considering the question carefully she said, "No, it is not true. I mean, look at the response. Every time. The more me I am, the more they love it."

Denial dismantled. Three minutes.

Then I asked her, "And if you knew that the more full-out you are, the more they love it, how would you be with people?"

"Oh, well, simple. I would figure out what *I* think, say it clearly, from my heart. I would visit the departments and the teams with full energy, and I would speak with good volume and be as funny as I like to be."

Florence kept the Incisive Question with her for a few weeks, until she did not need it any more. She lived full-out so much more of the time, and with others praising her as she did. The reluctant, de-energized Florence almost disappeared.

Reality recovered. Two weeks.

Pretty good for the demise of a 50-year-old tenacious and loud childhood god: "Don't be too much, step back, fade a bit, people won't like you if you stand out." Children eventually believe nonsense like this, these gods, these assumptions. They have to. They have to choose between trusting their own perceptions and keeping their parents' perceptions pristine. They only grudgingly give up the latter. They seek to see their parents as right, for as long as they can.

Denial is powerful. And until it gives way to a grown-up look at reality, at real information, both bad and good, it sabotages good thinking. At any age.

Thinking dies in denial. Information resurrects it.

CHAPTER 9

What Is The Matter With Us?

Feelings

Allowing appropriate emotional release to restore thinking

Fear constricts everything especially thinking

Crying can make you smarter

After laughter thinking improves

It is the oddest thing. Someone speaks; we are fine. Someone laughs; we are fine. But someone cries, and we are not fine. And let five sobs and a wail escape from a person's throat, and we get very nervous. What is it about tears that makes us crazy when they start?

And it is not just the recipients of tears who behave this way. The producers of tears freak out, too. The very second we can tell that our own tears are hovering, we apologize. I am so sorry, we say, flying for a tissue that is surely somewhere in the bottom of this bag. I am sorry. For what? For doing the thing nature intended us to do when we surface painful feelings so that we can think better? Why would we apologize for that? Surely that is stupid. Culture has a lot to answer for.

Maybe we can change culture. We could start with this simple observation: When someone cries, everything is fine. Really.

In fact, everything has just started to get really fine. Especially the person's thinking.

Stewart started talking. He was the Chairman of the Merger Integration Committee. People liked him. They also respected his leadership. And he met all of the requirements for being a real man. He was tall, fit, former Captain of his championship football team, current winner of the regional triathlon, youngest ever Vice President in the company, father of two, husband of one. And on this day he was about to turn some culture upside down.

"As you know," he said, "as part of the integration process, we have decided to speed up the forming of my new executive team. I find this very difficult. You are a fine team. You have out-performed all projections. You have worked together like a fine chamber ensemble. It feels wrong to me at some level that this much excellence should be dismantled."

He looked around the table. He looked right into the eyes of each of the ten people. They had worked together for two years. People said in fact, that had every team's performance been as good, the Board would not have sought another company to buy.

"So I want to say something about each of you. I want you to go on to your next position with this truth in your heart and mind."

He began with Liu. He looked at him. He had seen this young man take on gigantic projects. "You have taught us all, Liu, how to be human with inhuman demand."

Tears emerging, he continued around the group, eloquently. He saw tears in other eyes, too. And no one covered their face or squirmed in their chair. Stewart had said that people think better if they can cry.

He had also taught them about endings and about the work of Vanessa Helps of the company Going Well. They all knew that there are deaths of many kinds and that all deaths, even the death of a team, can register in the human body as loss. In this case, loss was certainly what Stewart and everyone around that table would go through over the next two months or more. Tears today were acts of rationality.

"It was good for us to feel this transition at its hardest," he said to me later. "We thought better later in the meeting about how to lead the rest of the company through the integration. And we noticed that the teams that just watched the hatchets fall among them, severing more than departmental limbs, hearts as well, reported difficulties for over a year. Some never committed to the new company."

Stewart led, and with his leadership he dismantled two cultures at once. He was a man. And he cried. When leaders lead by destroying destructive culture, they lead us to more than business success. They lead us to human freedom, including the freedom to think.

Crying can make you smarter.

Who Is Afraid?

Grief is not the only feeling our cultures forbid. We do not like fear either. True, you may say. But actually, you may ask, who is afraid?

Everyone. Everywhere. You are afraid. Everyone around you is afraid. Most decisions, including the big organizational ones, emerge from fear. Most policies, most systems, most regimes, most strategies grow out of fear. Nothing is more prevalent throughout our days and nights than fear. But nobody says so. Nobody owns up. Nobody even speaks the word.

And what are we afraid of? Surprisingly, not so much the obvious, like death, or shootings, or bankruptcy or cancer. But quieter things. Things like failure. Like humiliation. Like being wasted. Like exclusion. Like having no dreams. Things that rip up dignity.

Fear is so prevalent and so forbidden that it eats away at our thinking much of the time. And that thinking forms the structures of our relationships and systems. Everything shows the fault lines of fear.

We need to admit it. We are afraid. Then we need to talk about it. And feel it. And then we need to ask ourselves, "What are we assuming that is making us afraid?" And then we need to build Incisive Questions to remove the fear and replace it with sound, sensible, scintillating thinking. We will explore just how to do that in a little while.

And of course we also need to change our own behaviour that frightens people. They cannot think around us when they are afraid. Jane would have done well to understand this.

Feel Your Feelings But Trust Your Instruments

There is another dimension to this Component of Feelings. It is not as simple as saying, "Emotional Intelligence is in. Stoicism is out. Feelings are now okay. Express them anytime." Expressing feelings is okay sometimes. That is, they are there to be experienced, not repressed or demeaned or denied. But sometimes they arise in situations in which expressing them is dangerous – dangerous to good thinking. (Again, consider Jane's meeting.)

Ideally, the minute painful feelings arise, we can express and release them, and let that lead to better thinking. But ideally isn't always. In fact, ideally is hardly ever. And so we need to build an intelligent relationship with our feelings that allows us to know when to act on them and when not to, when to stop right there and release them, and when to wait.

Let's say that you are in a group. Someone says something. It enrages you. You strike at them. You say later that you were being authentic, human, honest. You felt rage. You expressed rage. What is wrong with that?

Only one thing. People stop thinking. And so do you. Rage silences. So, if silence is your aim, rage on. But that silence is only survival. It is not reply. It is not even compliance. It is fear. And things, especially human minds, freeze in fear. And if you have flown over Alaska, you know that not much thinking goes on in those blue glacier veins. And they take a long time to thaw.

So let's go back for a moment to that meeting. Someone said something. It enraged you. Now what do you do if people's thinking, rather than their survival, is what you want from the meeting? You trust your instruments. In fog, you trust your instruments. And fog is exactly what you are in when rage walks toward you, puckers its lips and curls its finger in your direction.

In fog you have to remember that *after* you land the plane, you can run to the lavatory and scream, or call your coach or therapist or best friend or haul out your journal and let rip. But in the fog, 1,000 feet up, 25 miles from the runway, you trust your instruments. The "seat of your pants" won't do. Trusting your feelings in fog is the best way possible to crash. Up is down. Right is left. Not pretty.

My twin brother, a C141 pilot, taught me this viscerally one day. He put me in a large swivel chair, one I could fold my legs into and lean back in. He asked me to close my eyes. He said he would spin the chair around, and that I was to tell him when he had reversed the direction of the spin. And then I was to tell him again when he had reversed it back in the original direction.

I closed my eyes and began spinning, and soon I sensed that the chair had slowed down and was gradually beginning to reverse direction. When I was certain that I was now spinning right when I had been spinning left, I said so.

"Okay," he said. "Now say when you think I've changed it back."

The same thing happened. I sensed the chair's loss of velocity and then I could sense its change of direction. I said so. Bill said, "OK, now open your eyes."

"Was I right?" I asked.

"No," he said, "I never changed the direction of the spin."

I could not believe it. I was sure he was kidding. But then I tried it on his daughter, Laura, and the same thing happened. I never changed the direction, and she thought I had three times.

So, in the meeting, when your rage rises, notice the fog coming in. Summon interest, compassion, logic, ease and a personal commitment to every mind in that room – and to the future of your relationships with each of those people – and to the finest possible outcome from the discussion. Trust your instruments.

Your instruments are saying, "Every person here is inherently good, intelligent, loving and creative. That includes you. You are loved. You matter. You are not in danger. Kindness, clarity, ease and genuine interest will send those minds toward that solution. If you knew that you can say what you think in such a way that they can think about it well, what would you say next? And how would you say it?"

These perspectives, these thoughts, are your instruments. Your instruments are your feelings' best friends.

So, the list of The Ten Components includes feelings for two reasons: 1) the benign ones help us think better, and 2) the painful ones can be released in the right circumstances. Human beings come ready to handle feelings, not just to have them. Human beings, alert to their feelings, can choose what to do with them.

And not all feelings are painful. Some are gorgeous. And expressing those helps us think. After laughter, for example, thinking improves. So if you are a leader, before you do one other thing today, dig around and find your sense of humour. And not the kind that hurts people. The kind that perks people up. The kind that snaps everything back into perspective, and buttresses the best in people. The kind that makes people want to be with you.

So we need to master this Component of Feelings, this finely calibrated wondrous part of being human. Then we can produce an equally wondrous ensemble in the thinking around us.

CHAPTER 10

Who Are You Really?

Diversity

Encouraging divergent thinking

Ensuring diverse group identities

The mind works best in the presence of reality

Reality is diverse

Our Powerful Years Workshop began like this:

> *Welcome each of you to this Powerful Years Workshop, focusing on the truth about women and age. Let's begin there, with the truth. Around this table is intelligence. Around this table is influence and leadership; invaluable resource for our world and dreams unfolding.*
>
> *Those would not be interesting statements if all of us around this table were 26 years old. But because all of us around this table are between 40 and 77 years old, those statements are controversial, and, to some, threatening.*
>
> *This is because also around our world is the injunction to lie about this – and to believe, live, invest in and pass on those lies. The parts of our society that seek to keep a few people privileged and powerful also seek to convince women over 40 and absolutely over 50, 60, 70, 80, 90 that as we age, we are increasingly ugly, stupid, unimportant and at the end of our dreams.*
>
> *Around this table each of us alternately rejects this message, struggles with this message, believes this*

message and denies this message. Some days are better than others.

Today we want to think about all of this. We want to take another step in freeing ourselves from the lies, and re-instating the truth. Each of us has different issues about age. Each of us has different stories, different goals. Today we want to establish the best possible environment in which to do our best thinking about these things.

My passion for this topic took full form in the middle of a coaching session. My client, Sigrid, was devastated. She had decided to campaign for a national office. She had ten years of political experience and a robust following. And she was bright. And beautiful. That day she had been on a TV panel of candidates. The commentator asked, "Sigrid, how can you in good conscience put yourself forward for high office again? You are now 50 years old. What can you possibly offer?"

Sigrid answered with her usual acuity and warmth and power. "I will answer that," she said, "with a comment and a question. First, I have to offer intelligence, experience, a ten-year track record of exceptional political success, values our country needs in leaders, knowledge and courage. And my question is, 'Are you going to ask the men on this panel the same question?'"

She got through it. But she was shattered. "I am losing my self-confidence," she told me. "I don't know what to do. I am furious, of course. But under that I am frightened."

The session led eventually to this Incisive Question:

If you knew that everything about you, especially your age, is perfect, how would you feel, and what would you do next in the campaign?

One of her answers to the question led her an hour later to the office of the commentator. She and he carved open the issue of women over 50. "It is like racism," she told him. "Except that it is sanctioned. And anti-aging prejudice makes more money for the pharmaceutical research industry than heart and cancer research combined." He apologized. She went back on the trail. She won.

The damage to her campaign was negligible. The damage to her confidence was potentially serious. And that is because from the minute we start to age, which is the minute we are born, untrue limiting assumptions about our bodies, our intelligence and our importance enter our minds and take up residence like a genetic imprint, and we loathe this facet of our diversity. We fear the changes that come with age because of the assumptions that come with it without our permission: You are ugly, stupid, unimportant and at the end of your dreams. And it does not take much to release those assumptions into action. Then we become afraid.

That is the bad news. The good news is that we understand this. And we can do something about it. We can do this for every identity group that is part of who we are.

I did this with a group of male professionals once. We were exploring the fact that assumptions about people's group identities cause us to objectify them, to, as the Arbinger Institute says, "horribilize" them; and in seeing them as "other" we treat them as less than human. Replacing the untrue assumptions with true liberating ones helps us to think better with each other.

They first chose one of their group identities. Then they found the key untrue assumption that diminishes that group. Then they replaced it with a true, liberating one.

Take a look:

Group Identity	Untrue Limiting Assumption	True Liberating Assumption
Home educating families	Families who home-educate their children limit the children's development.	Families who home-educate provide a broader education than is possible in age-segregated classes.
Buddhists	Buddhists worship images.	Buddhist images are visual reminders of highly-regarded values such as wisdom and compassion.
Jews	The Jews killed Jesus.	The Roman Government killed Jesus.
Home-based business owners	Home-based business owners don't have what it takes to be successful.	Home-based business owners are the cutting edge of busines development.
Christians	Christians believe they have the exclusive road to truth.	Christians inherently respect and learn from other beliefs.
Entrepreneurs	Entrepreneurs are interested only in money.	Real Entrepreneurs create better solutions to life's problems.
Liberals	Liberals want people in need to receive handouts from people who work hard.	Liberals compassionately hold people responsible for making their lives work.
Middle-aged mothers	Middle-aged mothers must identify self through their children's accomplishments.	Middle-aged mothers are at the perfect stage to express more of who they really are.
Men	Men are inattentive.	Both men and women need to learn the art of Attention.

In addition to the chosen assumptions on the previous page, each person recognized that every identity group that is the target of prejudice shares also a common assumption: your thinking does not count. This assumption does the greatest damage. And because we internalize the assumptions, we stop thinking well.

In fact, that is why the definition of Diversity in a Thinking Environment is both diversity of group identity and diversity of ideas. When we don't value each other's identity differences, we don't value our divergent thinking. We worship at the altar of homogeneity. Actually, we sacrifice there. But this time it is no lamb that dies. It is human thinking.

Homogeneity sounds so nice. Same, comfortable, familiar, predictable. But it is ruthless. And it infects even our conception of how to slay it. "Welcome," we say. "We now value diversity. We want you. Welcome to our world. If you will be like us, you can join us. There is nothing wrong with you, as long as you look like, think like, act like, lead like, advance like, decide like, keep time like, create like, socialize like and consume like us. No problem. We have gotten over our prejudices. We now welcome you into us."

Assumptions of superiority, like cockroaches, are the last things to die. And along the way, thinking, real and diverse and innovative thinking, is stillborn.

It seems that when we can think *as* ourselves, we can finally think *for* ourselves. Until then we are trying to think like the people who hold open the door.

Diversity demands disarming degrees of disinvestment in sameness. Someday we will celebrate that daring. That day we will hear ourselves say, "Welcome, and please be the most *you* you can be. Think as *you*. Act as you. It is you we need."

And Diversity will finally have arrived in our midst – humble, warm, a giant bright light of a thing. And we will think together. All of us. As ourselves.

CHAPTER 11

Where Is Freedom?

Incisive Questions

Removing untrue limiting assumptions that are blocking thinking

Right inside an Incisive Question lies the liberation of the human mind

Assumptions drive everything. They drive the good. They drive the bad. This book, any book about autonomous thinking, must begin with a bold line under the starring role of assumptions.

Friends gave me a Morning Glory plant for my birthday. It was a stem and two leaves. The tiniest thing you have ever seen. But inside it somewhere, somehow, were purple, blousy, blossom-festooned, soon-to-be-galloping glorious things, hundreds of them. They were in there. Actually, it was not so much *they* that were in there, as the means to make them. And with just the right few external things to assist (sun, rain, soil), those two leaves and one stem would make a near universe of concrete, squeezable, veiny, fast-birthing, curvy, winding sequencings of colour and shape. And it would soon become impossible to find the stem and two leaves any longer.

It is all in there ready to go.

I set the tiny thing on the bench. In that second, I managed to be transported, as if I had never seen a plant before.

What is that process, I asked no one. What is all that bigness inside all that tiny-ness? What is it nature does to go from nearly nothing to masses of something, with no wand? Botanists understand. And these days we can just Google it. It is known, predictable and replicable; and as long as the sequence is allowed to unfold and the internal and external forces are working together just so, those glories will burst and sing and dance during the day, and tuck themselves tightly in at dusk, pretty much for the whole summer.

You can count on it. And it is no less wondrous because of that.

I thought of other invisible things, how they live right there in front of us, also ready to go. Breakthroughs in human thinking, for example. Actually, they are not even like that; they *are* that. They lie there, needing only a few perfectly calibrated external things, and suddenly they go into action.

This breakthrough process is every bit as predictable and learnable as the inside story of the Morning Glory. And, again, it is no less wondrous because of that.

You are thinking along. Ideas, clarity, insights are practically tumbling over each other. Then, no warning, you freeze. You can't move. You can't solve the problem. You can't get the next good idea. You can no longer understand. All so suddenly.

What has happened? An invisible thing has happened. An untrue limiting assumption *that you live as true* has walked onto the road. That's all. It is not that your wiring has blown, or you have become unlovable, or your coupons for success have expired. It is just an untrue limiting assumption, and it has erected itself across your path. No big deal, except that it is exactly the thing that stops good thinking all day, everyday, everywhere.

The other big deal is that most of us don't recognize it or know how to get rid of it.

Assumptions are not dry. They sound it, in the abstract, but in the actual they are glittering, terrifying, velvety, teeth-baring, piercing, rock-a-bye, grave, generous, power-hungry things. The presence of assumptions at the very core of our lives is actually an electrifying concept. And searching for them competes hands down with the best forensic thriller you ever couldn't put down. Promise.

For example, I could ask you right now, "What was the best decision you ever made?" You would know. Then I could ask you, "What were you assuming that led you to make that decision?" And you would know.

Equally, I could ask you, "What was the worst mistake you ever made?" And you would know. And then, "What were you assuming that led you to make it?" You would know that, too.

Or we could get less dramatic, and I could ask you, "What were you assuming that led you to open this book?" Or, "What are you assuming that keeps you in your current job?" Or, "What are you assuming that is making you feel happy, or worried, or un-confident, or relaxed?" And you would know.

How long could this list get? Long. Virtually everything we do, think and feel begins with assumptions. Maybe they don't drive the autonomic nervous system. But sometimes I wonder about even that. For instance, I have known women who said they wanted to die as soon as their husbands died. And when their husbands died, they did. They stopped their own hearts. The very day. Their autonomic nervous systems were certainly being driven by something other than the general state of their medulla oblongatas and their dinners.

Only a few things are truly automatic. Probably the flow of pancreatic juices and the slow creep of chin hairs are automatic. We can be assuming nothing and those things will just keep on rolling. Probably. But even the apparently out-of-our-control system of immune cell production seems alert to our assumptions. For example, if I assume that I am in charge of my life and do not have to say "yes" to people when I mean "no", really assume it, my lymphocytes and T helper-cells will proliferate in just the right numbers to keep me from nasty infections and cancers. (Read the medical research of Lydia Temoshok to be further enlightened on this amazing point.) So who is to say what assumptions do not control?

Assumptions are the reason we think, feel, decide and do just about everything. The excitement starts when we start noticing them, and then replace the untrue ones with true ones, and put the true ones into that particularly powerful kind of question, an Incisive Question, a construction the mind makes naturally, I think, anytime it can.

Nature's Breakthrough Process

The construction of this question may very well be the way the mind breaks through blocks. We call these natural, powerful questions Incisive Questions. They are essential to success in our lives. And we need to get good at them. And when we do, we become uniquely helpful.

Human beings have taken apart and seen the mechanisms of plants; but we have not done the same for the human mind as it, too, breaks through.

It is fiercely complex, this actual process of breaking through (neurologically, chemically, electrically speaking). But in practice, it is very simple. The mind simply constructs an Incisive Question for itself. It plays out like this:

You are thinking along. Again, suddenly, you make an untrue limiting assumption. You regard it as true. You stop. You can't go forward. But this time you get out. You walk around the assumption. You decide to question it. Is it true? You walk around it some more. You lie on the ground and look at it from toes to head. You thump it. You splash it. And you say, nope, it's not true. Factually, logically, philosophically it cannot be defended.

Well, you ask, if that assumption is not true, what are my words for what is true and liberating? You figure that out. You then ask yourself, "If I knew *that*, how would I go forward?" And pretty much abracadabra (except for the wand), the block (untrue limiting assumption) vanishes, and you continue down the road, ideas proliferating, feelings easing, ways opening.

That sequence of questions seems to be what the mind does naturally to break through blocks. The mind has always done it this way, but we have not understood it well enough. Now perhaps we are beginning to. And best of all, when the mind cannot quite do it internally for itself, we can provide two perfect external things to make it happen.

The external things are Attention and an Incisive Question. Here, in a simplified form (see Chapters 21 and following for the satisfyingly more complex sequence) is the sequence of questions that leads to the Incisive one:

> What are you assuming that is most stopping you from going forward?
>
> Do you *think* that assumption is true?
>
> What is true and liberating instead?
>
> If you knew (insert liberating assumption), how would you go forward?

For example, let's say you are thinking about an energy-saving light bulb that gives soft, creamy light, none of that bluey, cold, dead stuff. You have some decent ideas. Suddenly you don't have any more ideas, and the ones you thought of begin to seem unworkable. But you don't panic or go get a real job. You ask yourself, "What am I assuming that is stopping my thinking here?"

You know immediately. "I am assuming that once we create the bulb, no one will capitalize its production. And this is because we are too young, because when Steve Jobs went to Hewlett Packard in 1973 with the blueprint for the Apple personal computer, HP said to him, 'Go away, you haven't even been to college yet.'"

You are pretty exercised about what happened to Steve Jobs, but you step back from it for a second and you ask yourself, "Does that prove, so do I think it is *true*, that once I create the bulb, no one will capitalize its production?"

And you realize that you cannot defend the assumption factually, logically or philosophically. "Young people practically rule the world of innovation these days," you reason, "and anyway, the fact that it happened to Steve Jobs 30 years ago, does not prove it will happen to me. The past does not inherently determine the future. "So, no," you confirm, "the assumption is not true."

Then you ask yourself, "If it is not true that once I create the bulb, no one will capitalize its production, what are my words for what is true and liberating?"

And you know. Just like that. In *your* words. "The market for this bulb is gigantic." Definitely a true, liberating alternative.

And then you place that liberating true assumption into a question, "If I knew that the market for this bulb is gigantic, what ideas would I have next for the design?" And you are off again, creative as morning.

We call it an Incisive Question because it cuts through an untrue limiting assumption to replace it with a true liberating alternative. Seamlessly, thinking resumes.

Inside the human mind, invisible, but in front of us all of the time, lies this extraordinary breakthrough process, this sequence of questions that is so finely woven at first it eludes detection. But it is there. And we can offer it to each other anytime to re-open the road.

It is Incisive Questions that turn the mind's stem and two leaves into all that glory.

CHAPTER 12

Does It Matter That You Matter?

Place

Creating a physical environment that says back to people, "You matter"

When the physical environment affirms their importance, people think at their best

When we respect our bodies, our thinking improves

In my first job (at a then new Quaker school in the countryside of Maryland), teaching English and Latin, dance and hockey (well, they were desperate), I decided I needed some more classroom equipment. So I went to the headmaster's office.

C Thornton Brown was his name. We called him Thorny. But he was anything but prickly. Firm, but so gentle, his wisdom usually broad-sided you. I knew this from experience.

I knocked on his always-open door and saw him leaning back in his chair looking out at the Maryland October sky, a pearl in that part of the world. "Excuse me, Thorny, do you have a minute?" I asked.

"Sure," he said, bringing the chair and his attention forward. He smiled. And said nothing. Not one single extraneous word ever came out of that man's mouth. I knew from the moment I met him that I should learn that from him. But I gave up early on. The odds against success in some things in life are just too great.

I plunged in, "I need a few things for my classroom that will help me do a better job of teaching," I said. I smiled, following his example for what to do after being breathlessly succinct.

"Such as?" he asked.

"Well, I need a desk chair that doesn't wobble. And I need a nice wooden in-tray for letters and things, a see-through ruler and a blotter. Oh, and coloured chalk."

He kept looking at me and listening. But that was all I could think of to say. I had said what I needed, though not any of the reasons why, because they seemed obvious. Every teacher needed stuff like that. And anyway, it was that first semester when I was still trying out the idea of not going overboard in the talking department.

But he did not grant my request. Nor did he deny it. He took a long time to speak at all, but looked completely peaceful and fine. I thought maybe he was adding up the expense, so I thought about saying that I knew where we could get a used, but good, desk chair. I had seen one at the Thrift Shop down the road.

But something told me to wait. And, uncharacteristically, I obeyed. I smiled some more.

"Nancy, there are only four things you need in order to teach well."

I listened. I figured the coloured chalk was already a goner.

"You need students who want to learn. You need something worthwhile to teach them. You need profound respect for their intelligence. And you need to be sure they speak more than you do."

I kept listening. Differently this time. Somehow I knew that if I could ever really understand what he had just said, it would change my life. It was never straightforward going into Thorny's office.

"And," he continued, as gently as he had said the first thing, "You can achieve all of those four things sitting on a log in the woods."

And that was that. I didn't know whether that was a no or a yes. I did know that it was as good as divine.

It did change my life. I began to understand about learning. And without knowing it, I began to understand about Place. I understood that the Place of learning, of thinking, has very little to do with accoutrements and everything to do with an ambience that dignifies the thinker. And I was relieved that, as with all wisdom, sitting on a log in the woods was a metaphor. Snow in Maryland can get deep.

But, I came to interpret Thorny's words a few years later as this: When we are thinking, the Place needs to say back to us, "*You* matter." That is all. And that is everything. When we know that *we* matter, we think at our best.

So now when people choose spaces for thinking, for coaching, for meeting, if they want to help people to think for themselves well, they choose a physical Place that welcomes them, that in its simplicity and accessibility, and even, if possible, in its décor, whispers to them, "You matter."

And they make sure they talk less than the Thinker.

Recently we have realized that there is another physical Place that needs also to say, "You matter." It is your body. Your body is the place in which you do your thinking no matter where else you are. And so, it needs to be as healthy as possible, as robust, as guilt-free, as reflective as possible of your true self, of what you value and espouse. It needs to show that you respect it and take care with it and are not in denial about it.

When you sit down with yourself to think, you will think better if you are in a good relationship with your body. If you can face it with pride, knowing you are doing everything you know to do to show it that it matters, your thinking will improve.

Human lore has been saying this for a long time. "Your body is your temple." That is cliché now, and the punch is gone. But it means, "Your body is where you take place." It is where you think and feel and decide and act. It needs to be treated for that without-which role it plays in every second of your life.

Your body cannot be put off. It goes on generating your thinking, all during your procrastination to care for it; but the thinking that it generates reflects that procrastination. It has a kind of holding-pattern essence to it. It is not your best, not nearly.

So starting right now, considering acutely the state of your body. Is it fit for thinking?

And have you found just the right log?

What matters is that you matter.

Part Two

In Practice

In Pairs

CHAPTER 13

What's Wrong With Being Wrong?

The Essential Mistake

The mind works best in the presence of a question.

That observation is important to remember when your goal is good thinking. Especially independent thinking. And most especially when your goal is good thinking about good thinking. And if your goal is to improve the Thinking Environment you are creating, you have to *love* questions. You have to love questions more than answers.

And most of all, you have to love questions whose answers might prove you wrong.

The Thinking Environment is always revealing itself. It is our privilege (everyone's) to notice it. And the new things, those nuances, those turns in the road, have come into view because we are passionate about being willing to be wrong in order to get closer to being right. And because, as I said, we love questions.

Questions drive discovery. My favourites are:

How far can people go in their thinking before they need my thinking?

How much further than that can they go *for themselves*?

And how much further than that?

And then, how much further even than that?

What do people need in order to keep doing their *own* thinking?

My least favourite question is:

> How do I zealously cram the Thinking Environment
> process into this moment with this person, and then ignore
> the fact that the seams have split, just so I don't discover
> that I might have been wrong for 25 years?

Being wrong is good. As long as you recognize it, and peer at it, and turn it over and upside down, and think with people about it, and spend some time in the bathtub wondering about it. And then seeing a new way forward.

If, on the other hand, you move on as if you were right when you are not, being wrong leads to the collapse of all the specious pieces.

The joy of being the good kind of being-wrong comes from desire. The desire to get as close to *actually* right as you can. That desire has to be pretty hot. There aren't a lot of people standing around you saying, "Risk being wrong; wrong is your road to right." Most voices are saying, "Never risk being wrong; wrong is your road to failure."

So people can be forgiven for not having their eyes peeled for their own mistakes.

But independent good thinking is scarce. And so re-thinking our fear of being wrong is pretty important.

The history of the Thinking Environment is a landscape more spectacular than the sea in Ikaria. And that is because the Thinking Environment welcomes mistakes. In fact, you could say that in the journey to determine what it takes for people to think for themselves, mistake-noticing is the key ticket. When the map gets smug, we throw it out.

We keep doing what works well, while we keep watch for what, this time, might not work so well. We watch for the thing that is in front of us that is not accounted for in the evolving theory, for the thing we would rather not see. We watch especially for infantilization – the act, usually in the name of support, of treating people, (including children) like children. Even though we are nearly obsessive about cleaning out every infantilization femtosecond from every Thinking Environment moment, the little suckers still sneak in all the side doors and sneer. Snatching them from this process is a full time job.

We can keep creating Thinking Environments for people only if we make ourselves enjoy noticing what works because of the questions that reveal what doesn't. We do well to embrace this principle:

> To ignite independent thinking in people we must be more
> drivingly interested in what the person really thinks than
> we are frightened of being proved wrong.

I think of this discovery process as being a bit like DNA in that way. Lewis Thomas said it eloquently in his magical book *The Medusa and the Snail*, in the chapter called, "The Wonderful Mistake":

> The capacity to blunder is the real marvel of DNA.
> Without this special attribute, we would still be anaerobic
> bacteria, and there would be no music.

So, to take us into our exploration of the sequence of questions that seem to replicate the mind's natural breakthrough process – The Thinking Partnership – let's take a look at the scariest possibility. If we are wrong about this one, we have some serious re-grouping to do.

CHAPTER 14

Are We Good?

The Positive Philosophical Choice

Actually, so far so good.

From the first searchings for the Thinking Environment, one assumption has loomed. It is the heart of the theory. And every artery depends on it. It is the assumption that human beings are inherently good. And intelligent. And imaginative. And capable of choice and of solving problems. And needing love – both to give it and to get it. And able to do both. Basically, the philosophical choice we make when we are helping someone to do their own thinking is that they are that marvellous. Inherently.

Inherent is the key term here. They may behave like pre-Neanderthals with no larynx and thus no language, and probably not lots of concepts or calculations. They may do even worse and hurt people for a living; or just be sophisticated victims at the bottom of life's executive pond. But when it is your job, or privilege, to help them think for themselves, you file their behaviour under consequence, and assume they are, inherently, deep in there somewhere, good, smart, full of choice, imaginative and keen not to hurt people.

But is it true?

Well, Socrates thought so. Among his many ideas that enraged the state and led to that unfortunate hemlock experience was this:

Human beings do not do wrong-doing knowingly.

Human beings, in other words, inherently strive for good and do bad things only because their thinking has become distorted, so that what is bad they think is good. Even our worst thoughts and actions,

Socrates would suggest, can be explained by poor thinking, which is a consequence of ignorance, neglect, misinformation, pain and deprivation of experience.

Arguments about this point have determined only that inherent nature is hard to determine. Psychologists have not been for ages in the throes of the nature/nurture debate for nothing. It is tricky. How do we know for sure what we are hard-wired to do and be, and what we are not?

If you want to join that debate, get a very large bucket of popcorn and settle in, because you are going to be a lot older when it is over. But if you want to get on with your life and work, and make a huge difference in a short time, choose the assumption about human nature that gets the best results. (And go back to the debate periodically to keep current, and in case it peps up.)

For all these years that is what we have done. We have chosen the view of human nature that produces the best independent thinking from people. That is why we call it a choice: The Positive Philosophical Choice. (That is a mouthful, I admit. But I was willing to go only so far in agreeing to acronyms and initials in this work. You just can't reduce something as profound and fundamental as The Positive Philosophical Choice to the PPC, can you? So you can use your amazing larynx, and enjoy the term.)

Are we good, inherently? Who knows? But when you want to think well, especially to do your *own* thinking, you will do it much better if I assume you are. You will be able to see those positive assumptions in my face, in my eyes, in my posture. You will be able to hear them in my (very few) words and sounds. You will be able to spot them particularly inside the Incisive Questions I ask you. You will know what I am assuming about you. If I assume you are as smart as anything, and capable of new ideas and authentic feelings and streamlined, just-right actions you have never before had an opportunity to generate, you will amaze yourself. You will in practice be that good. And it is the practice, the result, that makes our philosophical choice for us when Thinking Environments are our aim.

This is not a mysterious process. It is not that my mind goes into your mind making you smarter, woo woo. It is that if I assume you are intelligent and good, your inherent assumptions that you are intelligent and good will be encouraged to prevail. (See Carl Rogers' "Unconditional Positive Regard", for his take on these inborn positive assumptions). From those assumptions your mind will work better. If, on the other hand, I assume you are not so intelligent and not so good and need me to think for you, your mind will have to climb over that, stealing time and energy from your thinking.

And the chances are that your mind will let the negative assumptions from me mingle too much with the positive assumptions you were born with. The negative ones will usually begin to muscle in. This is because for most of your life society has been pouring in those negative assumptions, so there are a lot of them gurgling around in there.

Now, the brain is a breathtaking design. Way out of our grasp of understanding as yet. But it also is fragile. It seems to allow in a lot of bullies along with the beauties and let them box it out without a very good ref. So if I add more to the bully corner, the gentler liberating assumptions sometimes cower. The limiting ones kick them over and stand on their chest. And then the limiting ones form your ideas. Your not so great ideas.

Our thinking seems to be free proportionate to the freeing nature of our assumptions.

So it is truly important for me to choose the assumptions about your nature that will mirror with your own inborn positive assumptions so that your fine thinking can get on an impressive roll, and stay there.

The Positive Philosophical Choice is that influential.

And it is the results over these many years, the stunning and worthwhile thinking, that make me not worry that the Philosophical Choice is wrong. It may be. It may turn out that human nature, deep in our DNA, is rotten. But I doubt it. We do too many magnificent things to be so decayed at the core.

But anyway, maybe we aren't sunk if we turn out to be wrong about human nature. We simply will have to figure out how to explain in some other way the phenomenon of brilliance that arises when we assume that human beings are by nature a cluster of good things. Finding that explanation might be fun, actually. It might, though, require quite a few baths.

CHAPTER 15

Whose Turn Is It Anyway?

In Practice: In Pairs

So, we assume we are good. All of us, all of the time – inherently. Specifically, we assume we are intelligent, able to think through and solve anything. We assume we have choice. We assume we are loving and lovable. We assume that inherently we all want things to be right for everyone. And that our feelings are part of thinking well. And that we have a right to happiness. We assume, most of all, that we matter, equally.

We recall all Ten Components.

We are ready.

You speak. I listen.

Then I speak. You listen.

Then you speak. I listen.

Then I speak. You listen.

Perfect.

But when was the last time that happened?

Usually, you speak. I interrupt.

I speak. You scramble, smarting from the interruption. You interrupt.

You speak, rushing. I interrupt again.

You pause, seeking your just-right word. I interrupt with mine.

You take it, you growl, you use it, lose track of where you were headed, find another route, feel it isn't quite it. You pause. I grab the silence and speak.

You wince. I continue. You interrupt.

What is happening here? We are doing the most normal thing in the world: we are having a conversation, or even a professional session of some kind.

But what is wrong with this?

What is wrong is that neither of us is behaving as if we are remotely interested in what the other thinks. And neither of us has any idea what will generate best thinking from the other. Day after hour after meeting after session after interview after conversation after consultation, we do this. Somewhere inside we know it doesn't work. But we do it again anyway. Maybe it will work this time. But it never does.

This is because we have not asked ourselves two questions:

Do I *want* to know what this person really thinks?

And do I know how to help them think at their best?

We are unaware of an important thing: human beings communicate in structures. Even the most so-called spontaneous, freewheeling exchange between people is a structure. And it is often not too far from the scenario above. You could I guess call it the control and interruption structure. It looks loose. But it is actually a tight structure. And the chances it will build fine thinking between people are nearly zilch.

There are other structures, though, that do build good thinking. Some are in pairs. Some in groups. They work. They produce good thinking. And they produce lithe spontaneity.

In this part of the book we will explore 13 of these structures, 7 in pairs and 6 in groups. And we will see the ways they affect (and effect) finest thinking between human beings.

We will start with the Thinking Partnership structure because, as we have seen, it seems to replicate the mind's natural breakthrough process.

But first we need to decide – and it is a re-iterative decision – to want to know what people think. We need to be truly, madly, deeply *interested* in what they think, and in what they will think, and say, next. If we aren't, the other structures crash in with their AK-47s, and we find thinking globules on the walls.

So, do you? Do you want to know what people think? Do you want to know what your clients think when they are paying you to be the expert? Do you want to know what your colleague across the table thinks? Do you want to know what your child thinks? Your partner? Your students? Your patients?

Deciding to want to know, being interested, is the first step in their being able to do it brilliantly around you.

Actually, if you don't want to know what people think, become a hermit. At least there you are not pretending to generate good ideas, to make good decisions, to produce good action.

But if you are going to be with people, to have conversations, to have meetings with outcomes, to explore and debate, to create, to take humanity forward in whatever shy or shining ways, consider the structures of your interactions. Become conscious of the impact they are having on the delicate-robust human mind.

And consider the innate splendour of the mind's own structures.

As you do, you are sure to watch the individual human heart enfold the gigantic, human intellect, grounding us in what is real and launching us into what is possible.

CHAPTER 16

How Does Nature Do It?

The Thinking Partnership

The Thinking Partnership Session is mighty. It moves nearly mountains nearly always. And that is, I think, because it mirrors what the mind wants to do. It is what the mind does in a flash when it can. The Thinking Partnership Session is a sequence of questions, replicating the questions the mind seems to ask itself as it breaks through from blocks to brilliance. The Thinking Partnership Session simply re-constructs this natural process step by step.

We can offer this sequence of questions to each other when stunning levels of Attention have not yielded results quite stunning enough.

We have discovered lots about this natural process over the past nine years. I hope you will enjoy the greater thoroughness the Session now represents. Its complexity feeds the Session's simplicity.

So now in this section, moving from theory to practice, exploring work in pairs and then in groups, we start with the Thinking Partnership because every other application derives from it.

And because if it is extraordinary results you are after, this is one almost certain way to get them.

CHAPTER 17

What Does It Take?

Thinking Partnership Expertise

We watch Nureyev leap. We think, "Beautiful." Maybe we even think, "Wow." But we probably don't think, "That took a 70° external rotation on the sagittal axis, a shift from sensory to vestibular feedback, intake of 6 millilitres of water per kilo of weight per hour, perfect polymetric contraction, 20 years of stretch of the quadriceps femoris, 6 production departments, a $5,000 costume and 2 ounces of base makeup. Sure, it was beautiful. But really."

We admire what we see. But we don't see what we admire. It is all there. But it is invisible, when it is that good.

So is the work of a Thinking Partner. We watch it. We think, "Good." Maybe we even think, "Amazing." But we probably don't think, "That took generative Attention; riveted interest in what the Thinker will say next; courage to trust the Thinker's intelligence; awareness that the Thinker is the expert; warmth; mastery of the mind's natural breakthrough process; competence in summoning logic, information and a positive philosophical view of human nature to determine the truth of an assumption; being more interested in what the Thinker really thinks than we are frightened of being proved wrong; internal ease; comfort with the Thinker's silence; 60+ hours of practice; a place that says, 'You matter'; and humility. Okay, it was remarkable. But really."

Really is exactly the word. Those results do really take all of that. And it is all there. Almost all invisible. One simply breathtaking leap. And inside it a masterpiece of competence.

As with the Morning Glory, sometimes we do not know a work of art until we take it apart. Then seeing it as a whole again, we are transported by it all the more.

CHAPTER 18

How Much Further Than That?

Part I

How far can you go in your own good thinking before you need mine? How much further can you go than that? How much further than that? And how much further even than that?

As you know, those are the questions I think should be driving us as we help people think. Even if they have come to us asking explicitly for our help. Help is a funny thing. We usually think of it as giving people ideas and suggestions. But real help is giving people the framework in which to generate their own ideas first.

"What would you like to think about," Don asked Lucy, "and what are your thoughts?"

"Waste," Lucy said.

Lucy and Don, colleagues at an ad magazine, started their days, three times a week, this way. They gave each other ten minutes to think.

"Waste?" Don thought. "Nice morning topic. Not." But he kept his eyes on Lucy's eyes, and his face relaxed. This was simple. But for Don it took some doing.

Lucy continued. "I am trapped. I like this company, and I love writing and commissioning new pieces. But I have kind of plateaued. You know? I am not old, but I feel over."

She looked at Don.

He nodded, supporting her pace.

"When I was seven years old, I already wanted to be a journalist. I wrote down things people said and put them into stories. Then on some

Saturdays I went out to Dad's tool shed and greenhouse and pretended to be an editor of a big newspaper.

"I spread butcher paper over Dad's work bench. I called it *The Sentinel Star*. I wasn't sure what a sentinel was, but I had seen a newspaper called that, and I loved stars, so I figured it was the perfect thing.

"I wrote stories on it about people. I outlined them with twirly borders. Then I wrote a huge headline that would get everyone's attention. One I remember was, *Child Drowned in Backyard Well*. That was about my cousin.

"I put a stepladder under the high-up window, step by step carried tiny pots from the greenhouse up the ladder and set them on the windowsill. Then I climbed the ladder again with *The Sentinel Star*, leaned out the window and pretended to sell a pot with every newspaper.

"Streams of imaginary people came by. Everyone bought a newspaper and took home a clay pot. They were all fascinated by the articles and nearly ran into each other reading as they walked away.

"Those were my favourite Saturdays of my whole life.

"I don't know what happened to that energetic entrepreneur," she said, "but I want her back."

She paused. "That's all," she said.

Don asked, "And what more do you think, or feel, or want to say?"

She looked out past Don and through the window to something invisible.

Then she looked right into Don's eyes and said nothing. A rush of uncertainty washed over him, and he almost blurted out something reassuring like, "You are still as great as that little girl, Lucy." But just in time he remembered not to wreck her silence.

But Lucy was busy, and he trusted that.

"I was happy then," she said. "I sometimes spent all afternoon in that tool shed and never got bored. You know what I mean?" She asked.

"Definitely," he said, keeping it short.

"Yeah, well, I miss that little girl. So, Don, how do you get back the seven-year-old bouncy entrepreneur, sower of sunshine, when you are a seasoned storm-watching forty-five-year-old?"

"Rhetorical," Don thought. "Anyway, it's just as well, because I have no idea how you resurrect a seven-year-old kid steeped in fantasy play, and splice her into a done-this-too-long executive to come up with a released and fulfilled woman."

So he nodded as Lucy went on.

"So here's the deal," she said. "I produce this award-winning magazine. I do interviews with ad people. I have lunch with ad people. I report on trends of ad people. I am sick of ad people.

"I make good money. But something is wrong. I mean wrong for me. Wrong for *The Sentinel Star* editor. I am being wasted.

"So there. That's done. It sucks. But it's true. I do not want to be wasted one more minute."

Don wanted desperately now to stop listening and do something that felt like doing something. Every professional sinew in his body wanted to jump in and release her from her self-made cul-de-sac.

But they had agreed not to do that. They had agreed to give each other maximum chance to think for themselves before offering insight or direction. He re-decided to trust her intelligence.

Suddenly she was listless. "That's it," she said. "I'm done."

"And what more do you think, or feel or want to say?" he asked.

"Interesting," she said. "I just thought about our visit to Costa Rica. Lance took lots of photographs, and I wrote little articles from them. Sometimes they were political, sometimes intimate, like the moment between a dragonfly and the tip of an iguana's tongue."

"Not so intimate," Don thought, as he pictured the precarious, iridescent insect and the ghoulish reach of the reptile's tongue.

She was quiet for about 15 seconds. That is an eternity when you are dying to rescue.

"That is all I think," she said suddenly.

Don did not ask her what the hell Iguanas and dragonflies had to do with not being wasted at work; or whatever happened to the cute kid in the tool shed.

He asked slowly and gently, "What more do you think, or feel or want to say?"

"Nothing," Lucy said, "except that my brother became a nuclear physicist to get into the deepest level of existence, inside those subatomic quantum things. And my best friend became a priest to get into the deepest level of existence, inside the pulse before time, as she calls it. Somehow, in Costa Rica I got inside the deepest level of something. Me, I think."

Lucy turned her eyes away from Don. She was quiet. There was a longer silence then than he could ever remember not tampering with.

Then she said, "That's it! That's what I could do!" She beamed.

"And I would love it! And who knows, I might even be able to sell the Board on the idea as a new publication."

Don looked as affirming as a completely lost person could. Lucy nodded, smiling, finished. Don wanted to say, "Could you just fill me in here?"

But he decided again to trust her, so he lightened his tone and asked, "Well, what more do you think, or feel or want to say?"

Lucy did not hesitate. "I want to do what I did in Costa Rica. I want Lance to take pictures of unusual things in nature, and me to write stories, I want to create commentary on life in relationship to itself.

"Short pieces; gorgeous photos. Life in relationship. Things that would make people think about juxtapositions they never knew existed."

She was quiet for a few seconds. "And, we could help them see that relationship defines our existence.

"And the Board really might be interested. It is the kind of slightly wacko, wonderful thing they say they like. They said they want to use this company's publishing clout to get people looking at the world differently. So, why not?"

She looked back at Don. "That's all I can think of," she said, her eyes alert.

And he said warmly, "Anything more you think, or feel or want to say?"

Again the question worked.

"Why couldn't Lance and I publish something ourselves that would talk about relationships this way? Maybe a series of specialty books?"

Don recalled a phrase he had heard at a conference once: "The innovation glow." He figured he was looking straight at it.

Lucy smiled. "And I know just what to do first. I will write down my ideas and then talk with Lance about them tonight. Then we can make two business plans. Then I will figure out the next steps."

Don smiled.

"That's all," Lucy said. "That's great. Thank you. Now it's your turn."

CHAPTER 19

What Is He Doing?

Examining Part I

What happened there? Lucy changed her life. Don just sat there.

No, Lucy changed her life because, actually, Don did not just sit there. Lucy changed her life because Don *did* things. He spoke hardly at all. But he offered her Attention that is dynamic (as in dynamite). He caused explosions in her mind.

And when he spoke, he asked questions. Only two. He chose the questions that the human mind seems to need in order to keep thinking for itself. He had started with, "What would you like to think about and what are your thoughts?" And he followed up with, "What more do you think, or feel or want to say?"

All of his invisible riot of doing arose from those four questions I like so much:

> How far can you go in your own thinking before you
> need mine?
>
> How much further can you go than that?
>
> How much further than that?
>
> And how much further even than that?

Sometimes that is all it takes to free the human mind to find its own superb way. That is clearly all it took for Lucy that day.

(That, and of course, Don's regarding of Lucy as his *Equal*; and his internal *Ease*; and his implicit *Appreciation* of her ability to think; and his *Encouragement* of her by not competing with her; and his composure in the face of her own *Information* that she is being wasted; and his welcoming of the *Diversity* of their ideas and their identities; and his silent *Incisive Questions*; and his helping the *Place* say, "You matter" by booking – I forgot to tell you this part – Lucy's favourite conference room that day.)

All Ten Components were present during those amazing ten minutes. That is why it worked. And that is why we have to be ready to muzzle the mouths in our heads that are telling us to start working, to *help* this person, to be the expert here – to speak. To offer a solution, or to reflect back what she said, or to discuss her personality type, or to bring her back to her stated goal for the session, or to say what we think she is feeling, or to make a connection for her or to tell her what we see. Something! To ask a probing question at least. And one that is not just, "What more do you think?" The mouths in our heads are hard at it. But they are often wrong.

What the mind seems to need to think well is just what Don did. No more. Because that is transformatively, monumentally much.

And in a way, I think that if you were just to close this book now and walk out into the world and do what Don did, almost everything around you would change for the better. People would think better around you. And that would mean all round better decisions and quicker outcomes, and more significant conversations and more self-esteem everywhere, which would loop back to better thinking everywhere, too.

Of course, you would need to figure out your own, not-so-formal ways of asking those two questions. You don't want to sound like you just read a book about how to liberate the human mind. People who have just read books that propose big change have a kind of health-warning aura stuck to them. Others walk around them like a hole in the pavement. So make the questions yours. Just be sure your version invites them to think more – in their direction, not yours.

And do notice: Whenever you ask a person what they want to think about and then embody the Ten Components and then ask them what more they think, breakthroughs happen.

In fact, let's look at Lucy's breakthroughs. How did she, in just ten minutes, get from being wasted to starting a unique publication, without some clever input from Don? I think it was a journey something like this:

Lucy's mind noted what it wanted to achieve in the session: I want to stop being wasted.

Her mind noticed that it was blocked.

Her mind found the blocks – seven limiting assumptions:

I am trapped
I have to do this same job
It is stupid to leave a successful company
Little Lucy is gone
There is nothing wrong
The deeper me is accessible only outside work
I can make money on my new project only through my boss

Her mind figured out which assumption was most blocking her: I am trapped.

Her mind determined that the assumption was not true.

Her mind came up with a true liberating assumption to replace it: I can make a living doing the thing I love most.

Then her mind asked itself an Incisive Question with the liberating assumption as the focal point: If I knew that I can make a living doing the thing I love most, how would I stop being wasted?

And up came Lucy's own workable way to a new life.

Don sat there all right. He radiated interest and respect. And asked, "What more?" Five times. And embodied all of the other Components the whole time.

In doing this, Don ignited Lucy's mind. Specifically, I think that Don's Attention ignited those questions in Lucy's mind. When we say that Attention and the other Components ignite the human mind, maybe this is what we mean. We ignite *those questions* in the mind of the Thinker. And so it breaks through on its own.

We call this process *Part I of the Thinking Session*. And that is because it comes first. The trouble with the label, though, is that it seems to indicate that this Part is not enough, that the session is not complete unless it has other parts.

But Part I often doesn't need other parts, because actually it contains them all. Sometimes Part I is enough. And we need to be fine with that. But to be fine with it, we need to remember that it takes Nureyev-level expertise to make it happen. As the Thinking Partner, we *are* working; we *are* helping; we *are* being the expert. Impressively. Quietly. Generatively.

People all over the world, every hour of the day are looking for Part I. We need it to thrive. Maybe even to survive. We know that. And we don't know it, all at once.

It has been pounded into us not to need it, that it is selfish, indulgent, inefficient, incomplete, unnecessary, weak. But somewhere inside our smartest selves we know we need it, and need to give it.

Could there be any form of helping, any act of maturity, any offering of leadership, any road to a better world more straightforward to provide?

Part I. Let's do it. And when it is enough, let's rejoice.
And when it isn't, let's do what the mind needs next.
And we don't have to worry about what that is.
The Thinker will tell us.

CHAPTER 20

Are We There Yet?

Introducing Part II

Lucy was finished. Part I was enough. But it isn't always.

So how do you know?

You ask.

The Thinker, in order to keep thinking for themselves, needs now to reconnoitre, to take stock, to figure out what they want next. Only they can do that.

> What more do you want to achieve in this session?

That usually does it.

The Thinker will know the answer. And they will be right. And all of the things you think they should want from the rest of the session will often be wrong – because the Thinker is not you. By definition, we are likely to be wrong about what people need and want when we figure it out for them. So we get to relax here. It's nice.

When they answer the question, however, we go into gear. Their answer tells us what to do next. And, if their answer is anything other than "Nothing, I am finished," we have to hear – and memorize – their exact words. If their words are too numerous to memorize, we ask them to use fewer words. (This is not asking them to re-phrase or summarize it. Just to use fewer words. Their words matter. People think in their own words.)

> What more do you want to achieve from this session?

Now you might not imagine that there could be many different *types* of answers to that question. Many different answers, yes, infinitely. But types? Well, I didn't. But so far we have identified eight different types of answers, Further Goals, that emerge from that question. And the key thing about this arcane discovery is that the Thinker's answer, the type of Further Goal, tells you what to ask the Thinker next. The answer is the road map. Until that moment there was just horizon. And suddenly, with their answer and the clarity about what kind of goal it is, all kinds of signs and junctions and crossings and picnic areas pop up in front of you. This is nice, too, in a more demanding sort of way.

In a moment we will see what usually happens – when the Further Goal is what we call an Action Goal, and the main block is an untrue limiting assumption.

But for right now, take a look at these eight types of very distinct and fascinating Further Goals. It is interesting that even after thousands of sessions we find that the Thinker's answer to "What more do you want to achieve from this session?" is likely to be a request for one of these:

Eight Types Of Further Goals

1. Action Goal (to decide, to plan, to figure out, to compose, to maintain, etc)
2. Feeling Goal (to feel a certain way, to stop feeling a certain way)
3. Removing-The-Blocks Goal (to find the liberating assumption and build an Incisive Question)
4. Understanding-Why-I Goal (to understand why I think, feel or do something)
5. Looking-At-Assumptions Goal (only to unearth all the limiting assumptions)
6. Exploring-New-Topic Goal (to think about a topic different from previous Part I)
7. Activity Goal (to take action in the Session: writing, phoning, rehearsing, etc)
8. Information Goal (to find facts during the session)

Don't be daunted by them. When they show up, you will know. And you and the Thinker can discuss it if you don't know. The main thing is to recognize what the goal is saying about what the Thinker needs next. That tells you what to ask.

So here is Brian's session. His Further Goal was an Action Goal. Action Goals aren't always about action per se, as in leaping from tall buildings or making a cake. Action Goals are all kinds of doing, some of them on the abstract side. Brian's was "to figure out how to do the right thing". And, as always, it emerged out of Part I.

And by the way, the question, "What More Do You Want To Achieve From This Session?" is called Part II.

CHAPTER 21

What Is Right?

In Practice: Action Goal With An Untrue Limiting Assumption

Brian had determined that now was the time to act. He had seen corruption. He felt he could no longer remain quiet. Next Thursday there would be an inspection, and it would be his last chance.

In Part I of his session he had faced and faced again the implications of his silence.

"Janice goes home from work every night to danger," he had said, "because the Employee Rights Committee did not take action last year. I wrote the report about her husband's violence, but the Directorate deep-sixed it. Janice's husband is prominent. His donations to our organization are big. His position on the Commission got us our status. The whole sector loves him. It doesn't take Einstein to put the pieces together.

"And Janice has fresh wounds every week. Janice is bright. But her work now is dull. She seems further and further away."

Brian had finished there.

So Sean asked him, "What more do you want to achieve in this session?"

"I want to figure out how to do what is right," Brian said quietly, but firmly.

What Brian needed now was to find the block to that goal. Unless the block is lack of information, a need to cry or the lack of Part I and a Thinking Environment, the block to the Further Goal is usually an untrue limiting assumption. This is important to know.

And again, we don't have to guess at this. We just need to ask the Thinker.

So Sean asked, using Brian's words exactly, "What might you be assuming that is stopping you from figuring out how to do what is right?"

"I am assuming that if I re-surface the report and give it to the inspectors next Friday, I will be fired."

And allowing for, but not requiring, more assumptions to surface, Sean asked, "What else are you assuming that is stopping you from figuring out how to do what is right?"

"I am assuming that if I find a way to get the report to the inspectors surreptitiously, the staff will eventually know it was me who did it.

"I am assuming that this would be an act of professional betrayal.

"I am assuming that my shaky relationship with the Board will get worse.

"And I am assuming that there is no way to save Janice, and save my job."

"What else are you assuming that is stopping you from figuring out how to do what is right?" Sean asked again, just in case there might be more.

"That is all," Brian said clearly.

The mind thinks best about one thing at a time. So what Brian needed next to keep thinking for himself was to find the *key* assumption. And, as before, Brian was the only one who could make the choice. So Sean asked him, "Of those assumptions, or any that spring to mind, which is the one most stopping you from figuring out how to do what is right?"

"I think it is that this would be an act of professional betrayal."

The actual key limiting assumption is usually the untrue one. That is important to know, too. So Brian ultimately needed to explore whether or not his chosen assumption was true, according to the criteria of:

Information
Logic
The Positive Philosophical Choice

So Sean asked him, "Do you think it is true that this would be an act of professional betrayal?"

"That is hard," Brian said. "On the surface, yes. It would. I would be going behind the backs of the committee that covered up this report. I would be exposing them. They are my colleagues and my bosses. They would certainly see it as professional betrayal.

"But I don't know. It doesn't make sense that professional loyalty would perpetuate violence against a colleague. How can those two things exist side by side?

"So I wonder. What is loyalty? And to whom or what are we supposed to be loyal?

"And what is professional? Is it professional to allow a colleague to be beaten, and beaten down? I don't think so."

Brian was silent. A long time.

"No," he said, "it cannot be true. To rescue a colleague from danger is what matters here. It is all that matters. It matters even more than my job. Or my reputation among the staff.

"No," he said, "it is not true that this would be an act of professional betrayal."

"What are your reasons for thinking that it is not true?" Sean asked, perfectly.

"Well, it is unprofessional for the Directorate to have pulled the report and endangered Janice in the first place. In other words, it is not an act of professional betrayal to reveal an act of unprofessional behaviour."

Sean saw that his argument was logical and factual (and that the criterion of The Positive Philosophical Choice was not relevant with this assumption). The Criteria, therefore, agreed that Brian's assumption was untrue. He also knew that Brian now would need to find a true liberating assumption to replace the untrue one. So he continued smoothly, "If it is not true that this would be an act of professional betrayal, what would be your words for what is true and liberating?"

"Ah," Brian said, hardly drawing breath, "well, my revealing the truth actually restores our professional integrity; and so revealing it would actually be an act of professional loyalty. So, what is true and liberating is that it is professionally loyal to reveal this report."

Brian smiled and looked at Sean. Sean knew that it is not enough for the Thinker to understand the key assumption and to replace it with a true, liberating one. In order for their perspective to change, they need also to *experience* the liberating assumption. That happens best through a question. And Sean now had all of the words for that question. And every one of them was Brian's.

Sean asked him, "If you knew that it is professionally loyal to reveal this report, how would you do the right thing?"

"Amazing question," Brian said, looking away. He was silent for a while.

"I would take my copy of the report and read it again to be sure I am remembering everything correctly.

"I would then check through all of the case reports.

"I would then put my report onto a CD. I am on the welcoming group for Inspection Day, and I would give it to the Inspector as we shake hands. I would say, 'Please read this later. It is important.'"

He stopped. He was quiet again. Then he looked up.

Sean asked the same question again (adding the word "else") to help Brian generate more thinking, "If you knew that it is professionally loyal to reveal this report, how else would you do the right thing?"

More formed. "I would trust that good things happen in the end, and that if I am fired, I will find a better position with people of more integrity."

He stopped.

Sean asked again, "If you knew that it is professionally loyal to reveal this report, how else would you do the right thing?"

"I would pray for Janice. And be alert to her needs more than ever. I would tell her what I know about victims of violence and help her remember her own self-worth and innocence.

"I would plan with Anne a strategy for paying our bills for the months during which I might have to be finding another job. The good thing is that she will respect me for this, however hard it is for us for a while.

"And I would sleep soundly, something I haven't done much of for nearly a year.

"That's all," he said.

Sean asked again just in case. "If you knew that it is professionally loyal to reveal this report, how else would you do the right thing?"

"No, that's it. I am pleased. And I am tired.

"But I feel like a decent person again. Thank you."

I thought about something Gaby Porter said once after a Thinking Session, "It is a relief to let go of the noise – and face the music."

CHAPTER 22

Are We Having Fun Yet?

Examining Action Goal With Untrue Assumption

Surely that is beauty. Maybe Hopkins' "Spring" is more beautiful. But probably what is most beautiful about even that is the mind that produced it.

And that is the point, actually. The sequence of questions Sean offered Brian is not a contrivance, not a concoction. It is, we think, a close replication of the sequence of questions the mind asks itself (in Part I) when it can. When it can't, we do it for it. It takes longer. But it is nearly always that elegant, and the results nearly always that good.

We have chosen carefully the words to the questions. As accurately as we have figured out so far, they reflect the mind's own process. When the Thinker has an Action Goal, these are the questions their mind most likely wants to be asked. Here is a summary of Sean's version:

Part I
The chapter begins after Sean had asked the Part I questions:
1. What would you like to think about, and what are your thoughts?

2. What more do you think, or feel or want to say?

Part II
Then he asked the Part II question:
What more do you want to achieve with the session?

Part III

Then he asked the Part III questions appropriate for an Action Goal:

What are you assuming that is stopping you (from figuring out how to do the right thing)?

What else are you assuming that is stopping you (from figuring out how to do the right thing)?

What are you assuming that is *most* stopping you (from figuring out how to do the right thing)?

(Answer: That it would be an act of professional betrayal)

Do you think it is true (that it would be an act of professional betrayal)?

What are your reasons for thinking so?

If it is not true, what are your words for what is true and liberating?

(Answer: That it is professionally loyal to reveal this report)

Part IV

Then he asked the Part IV question – the Incisive Question:

If you knew (that it is professionally loyal to reveal this report), how would you (do the right thing)?

If you knew (that it is professionally loyal to reveal this report), how *else* would you (do the right thing)?

What Is The Truth?

The Three Criteria

Maybe you were as impressed as I was by the depth and speed of Brian's thinking when Sean asked him, "Do you think it is true that this would be an act of professional betrayal?"

Do you think it is true? We used not to ask that question. We just decided for the Thinker whether or not the assumption was true, and moved on to the next question. (Infantilization? No kidding. As I said, those suckers are sneaky. We were ages catching this one.)

And we debated. There was some heat in the debate, too. Because, yes, the Thinker does need to think about this for themselves, but who is to say what true is? Is the Thinker always right about what is true? Like if they say the key assumption is that they are stupid, and you ask them whether they think it is true that they are stupid, and they say "yes", and you ask what their reasons are, and they say that their mother told them they were stupid, and they made C's in geography and they spilled coffee into their keyboard.

Now, does that prove that they are stupid? Do we roll over and abandon them to that assumption and its illogical proof by agreeing with them?

No. That would really be stupid. But we were a long time figuring out what to do instead. Then one day it became clear to me in, you guessed it, a bath. An assumption seems to be true or untrue according to these three criteria:

> Information
>
> Logic
>
> Positive Philosophical Choice

"I am stupid," as it happens, aligns with none of these. The information to prove it was not true. The reasoning to prove it was not logical. And it does not fit with the Positive Philosophical Choice about the inherent intelligence of human beings.

So, no, it is not true that you are stupid.

Back to Brian. He thought hard about his assumption. Was it true that handing over the report would be an act of professional betrayal? It was in this part of Part III, in fact, that he seemed to have the most insight and to see the most deeply. He faced and saw through his fears, and he gained courage. This moment in the session was in itself hugely important.

And Sean did none of that work for him.

He did, however, listen carefully to the information, and to his logic, and keep in mind the Positive Philosophical Choice.

He saw that the Three Criteria agreed with Brian that the assumption was *not true*. So he proceeded to the next question – to find the true, liberating assumption. Perfect. Just what Brian's mind would probably have done for itself if it could have.

So that is one path through Part III: When the *Action Goal* is blocked by an *untrue limiting assumption*.

But sometimes the Action Goal seems to be blocked by a *true* limiting assumption. What does the Thinker need then in order to keep thinking?

That is when the real fun begins.

I remember when I took Wendy, my stepdaughter, to Maui. The first morning she woke me whispering, "Nancy, are we having fun yet? Or is it just me?"

So maybe I should ask you that question after we see what Jerome does with his Action Goal blocked by a true limiting assumption.

CHAPTER 23

So What?

In Practice: The Transition Question

"I want to make a plan."

Jerome was very clear. After Part I he was energetic.

"I feel good about my job now," he said, "and eventually I will move on. Both are true. Resolving what I could about the plan for that was important. But I still want to *make* the plan. I couldn't seem to do that just now."

"And so what is it you want to achieve with the rest of the session?" Rafi asked to be sure he had Jerome's own words. Freshening up the further goal in the Thinker's own words nearly always yields precision you would be sorry to miss.

"I want a plan to find a global position in a global organization."

Rafi's guess, "to plan for a big future", had not come close. He noted this.

Rafi knew three great strategic planning processes and two approaches to decision-making that he thought Jerome really should use at this moment. There was so much at stake.

But a deal is a deal. Rafi knew that Jerome expected him to help him find the blocks, the untrue assumptions, that were stopping him from making a plan. So Rafi moved on to Part III to find them.

"What are you assuming, Jerome, that is stopping you from making a plan to find a global position in a global organization?"

"I am assuming that I had my chance last year.

"That I won't find better than I have now.

"That I don't have what it takes.

"That I was lucky rather than talented before."

He stopped. "I am not sure about that one. Was I? Not sure. That might be the key one."

Rafi continued, "What else are you assuming that is stopping you from making a plan to find a global position in a global organization?"

"I am assuming that my CV has too many gaps.

"I am assuming that those gaps will hold me back."

Jerome nodded.

So Rafi asked again, "And what else are you assuming that is stopping you from making a plan to find a global position in a global organization?"

"That I don't know how to go about getting a role like this. And I think that's all," Jerome said.

"Anything else you might be assuming…?"

"Yes," Jerome broke in, "I am assuming that too much travel will be bad for me and Alice.

"And that I am a bad planner anyway, and that plans constrict you.

"That's all."

Glad I asked again, Rafi thought. That question generates things that just weren't there a second ago.

"Yes, that's all," Jerome confirmed.

"And of those assumptions or any that spring to mind," Rafi moved on, "which is the one *most* stopping you from making a plan to find a global position in a global organization?"

"That people may frown on the gaps in my CV."

"Do you think it is true that people may frown on the gaps in your CV?" Rafi asked, pretty sure he would if he were interviewing Jerome, but curious now where Jerome would go with this.

"Yes, I do," Jerome said. "My CV shows several spaces between jobs. I travelled then. I didn't work. I didn't get more experience in the industry. I think an employer might see that as flaky, or as time wasted."

Rafi saw that the Criteria would agree that the assumption was possibly true. He also knew that the Thinker, still in search of the untrue assumption, needs now to look inside the true one to find it.

So he asked the Transition Question, the question that finds the untrue assumption inside the true one.

The Transition Question

"It's possible that people may frown on the gaps in your CV, but what are you assuming that causes that assumption to stop you from making a plan to find a global position in a global organization?"

"Now that's a question. What am I assuming that causes the gaps assumption to stop me from making the plan? Okay, I think I am assuming that the gaps make me incompetent. Yes, that I am not competent for a global position because I had those gaps. Yes, that's it. I am assuming that I am incompetent."

"And do you *think* it is true that you are incompetent?" Rafi asked.

"Do I think it is true that I am incompetent?" Jerome thought for a moment. "Absolutely not," Jerome said with sudden fire in his voice. "Actually, it was those gaps that added to my leadership experience, to my understanding more about things that now make me more competent.

"No, I don't think it is true that I am incompetent because my job performance right now is tops, and if I were incompetent from the gaps I could not do the job I am doing now. Nope, not true."

Rafi noted that the criteria of Information and Logic agreed.

"So," Rafi said, "if it is not true that you are incompetent, what are your words for what is true and liberating?"

"Oh, that I have valuable varied experience," Jerome said as if it had been obvious all along.

"If you knew," said Rafi, putting all of that into an Incisive Question, "that you have valuable varied experience, what would be your plan to find a global position in a global organization?"

"Fantastic," Jerome said, "I would tell the story of the gaps differently. I would talk about them as a developmental experience, focusing me on what I want to do next.

"I would get that written up on Friday, with a colleague."

Jerome looked back at Rafi. "That's it," he said.

"And if you knew," Rafi asked afresh, "that you have valuable varied experience, what else would your plan be to find a global position in a global organization?"

"I would tell the CV story as a progression to being head of Learning and Development.

"I would also be clear what my global experience has been.

"And I would flesh out what this role I have in mind could look like.

"And I would remember that when the gaps got me the last time, the problem was in the way I explained them. It was not the gaps themselves.

"That's great, Rafi. I'm there. Now let's write all of this down. Ten minutes ago that plan was nowhere."

Rafi thought about the strategic planning sheets and the decision-making charts and scrunched them up in his mind. Nothing wrong with them, he mused. But something very right about this.

CHAPTER 24

What Is The Cause?

Examining The Transition Question

Good news.

We are not victims any more.

We might need a megaphone for this one.

Of course, if you have built your whole life around the notion that you are a victim, and are expert at being disappointed, and polished at blaming, and suspicious of things going your way for very long, this is going to be bad news. But then, again, I guess you could just be victimized by this news, and feel great (but not too great) about feeling bad.

Regardless, victimhood is out. Freedom is in.

This is because we now see that our true and possibly true limiting assumptions about life are not the problem. Sure, people might laugh at you. Sure, you might fail. Sure, so-and-so might not agree. Sure, it is a bit risky. Sure, you might cry. Sure, some people are better at this than you. Sure, no one has ever solved this problem before. Sure, she might leave. Sure, people might frown on the gaps in your CV. But that is not the problem. That is not the real block.

The real block is *inside* the true one. The real problem is the *untrue* limiting assumption smirking in there, arms behind its head, stretched on the lounger, shades on, Mai Tai on its way.

If the key assumption you choose first is true or possibly true, the actual key assumption is probably a different one. One that is *not true*.

We used to think that the key assumption was always a "Bedrock Assumption" (about the self or how life works). But we began to notice that sometimes the key assumption was not about either. Once in a while the key assumption was misinformation – the number of people coming is six, not sixty; there are four open positions, not one; the asking price was ten not one million, etc. So, whether Bedrock or not, the assumption we are looking for seems to be the key *untrue* limiting one.

Jerome found the untrue assumption fast. And that was great because he had been putting off, for ages, making a plan to find a global job in a global organization, all because he kept hurtling into that true assumption about the gaps in his CV. Ages. When all he needed to move it out of his way, in three minutes flat, was the gorgeous, de-victimizing, Transition Question.

I say gorgeous. *I* think it is gorgeous. It can take us from in-tow to in-charge in less than ten seconds once we let it in. That's pretty gorgeous.

But it is a teensy weensy bit un-idiomatic. And that puts some people off. But, oh my, it is worth getting because, well, freedom is worth a lot.

> That's possible, but what are you assuming that *causes*
> that assumption to stop you?

That's it.

Close your eyes. Try saying it.

How did you do?

Did you put the word "about" in it?

That's the challenge with this question. Idiomatically we want "about" to appear in the question. In our parlance if we say, "What are you assuming?" we follow the word "assuming" with "about". "What are you assuming about that?" we say.

But here "about" does not work. This is because the untrue limiting assumption we are looking for *rarely* is *about* the true one. It is about ourselves or life, or about just a small facet of the true one.

Jerome discovered this. Rafi asked, "It's possible that people may frown on the gaps in your CV. But what are you assuming that causes that to stop you from making a plan...?"

"I am assuming," Jerome said, "that I am incompetent."

"I am incompetent" was the untrue assumption. It was not about the people or the frowning.

The untrue assumption *causes* the true one to stop us. Put stars around that. The relationship is not derivative. It is *causal*.

Having fun yet? This is stunning stuff, actually. Just think about it.

"That's possible; what are you assuming that *causes* that assumption to stop you?"

That question finds the *cause*. It finds the untrue assumption that is *causing* the true one to stop us. And when we find the cause, we excise it; and we are free.

But as long as Jerome kept flattening in the face of, "People may frown on the gaps in my CV," he could not think. He was a victim. He could not make a plan. He did not know how to go forward. He felt bad. He was stuck. And he stayed stuck. That's what we do. We stay stuck in the face of a true or possibly true assumption. We are victimized by true assumptions because we think they are the block.

But the minute your Thinking Partner asks the Transition Question, you can see that actually something is lurking in there, an untrue assumption is *causing* the true one to stop you. An *untrue* assumption is the culprit. You then can replace that untrue limiting assumption with a true liberating one, connect it to your Further Goal through an Incisive Question, and you are off!

You make a transition from the true assumption to the untrue one. That is why we call it the Transition Question.

The relationship is causal. An untrue assumption *causes* a true one to stop us. So the question that finds the real block (the untrue assumption) uses the word "causes" is:

> That's possible, but what are you assuming that *causes*
> that assumption to stop you?

The Transition Question. Definitely gorgeous. Definitely fun.

Or is it just me?

I promise you, Maui is Pluto compared to the beauty and breeze of this question – after you master it, of course.

But, then, why wouldn't you want to master such a svelte act of human liberation?

CHAPTER 25

What If We Don't Agree?

In Practice: The Invitation Question

Maya was not fat. But she thought she was, and she thought about it all of the time. Her mother said she was "ample". Not comforting. Her boyfriend said he liked love handles. Sort of comforting. Not very. The medical magazines showed skinny girls who would soon die of not eating. Comforting in a twisted sort of way.

Maya had just graduated from medical school. She wanted to celebrate that achievement by figuring out how to stop thinking about her weight.

Celia thought that was a weird way to celebrate. But Celia's job for the next 30 minutes was to help Maya achieve her session goal, not to plan a party for her.

"So, can you say again what more you would like to achieve in this session?" Celia asked.

"I want to feel happy with my body," Maya said.

This, Celia noted, without much difficulty, was a Feeling Goal. This type of Further Goal is obvious because it has the word "feel" in it. Celia also already knew that the session would go all the way to an Incisive Question because most feelings (good or bad) emerge from assumptions. Incisive Questions use liberating true assumptions to get us to our goal of feeling the way we want to feel.

So on to find all the assumptions stopping Maya from feeling happy about her body.

"What are you assuming that is stopping you from feeling happy about your body?"

"Well, for one thing, I am assuming that thin is more beautiful than not thin.

"I am also assuming that people judge me for gaining weight and not losing it. That's the key one, actually."

"And what else are you assuming that is stopping you from feeling happy about your body?"

"That there is an inherent standard of beauty." She stopped. She looked at Celia.

"And what else...?"

"No, that's it. That there is an inherent standard of beauty."

Without rush Celia asked, "Do you think it is true that there is an inherent standard of beauty?"

Maya was quiet. "I am not sure," she said. "I don't want to. But, yes, I do think it is true that there is an inherent standard of beauty."

"And what are your reasons for thinking it is true that there is an inherent standard of beauty?"

"My experience. I experience beauty as being a certain thing. And my feelings. I feel that beauty is that standard.

"Also, I watch other people respond to a thin body. People love thin bodies.

"Also, you see that standard of beauty down the centuries. And in the movies.

"Also, I read in a study that newborn babies have a positive reaction to thin faces, and a negative reaction to fat faces. Or maybe it was to chiselled chins and high cheek bones. I'm not sure. Maybe it was to smiles, come to think of it. But anyway, yes, I do think there is an inherent standard of beauty."

Celia listened to those reasons. She considered the Three Criteria. "They don't align," she thought. "Maya's reasons don't prove that there is an inherent standard of beauty. They are not logical; there is no information to support the assumption; and the Positive Philosophical

Choice would definitely rule it out. According to it, every human being by nature is beautiful.

"So the Criteria and Maya disagree," Celia realized.

Tricky moment. More on the history of this moment later. But what Maya probably doesn't need now is a knock-down drag-out fight with Celia-as-Criteria. Also, she does not need to be abandoned to her untrue limiting assumption. And even though she cannot see that her assumption is untrue, what she does need in order to keep thinking for herself is to be freed from the grip of it.

One way for this to happen is for her to consider an alternative assumption that is *credible* to her. She needs what we call *The Invitation Question*. This is so far our best construction allowing the Thinker to move on from an assumption they consider true, but that the Criteria consider untrue. And without the huge shift in dynamic from in-charge to infantilization that the Thinker can experience in debate with the Thinking Partner.

Celia aced this. She said, "Given that the assumption that there is an inherent standard of beauty is stopping you from feeling happy about your body, what would you credibly have to assume in order to feel happy about your body?"

"What would I credibly have to assume?" Maya repeated quietly. "Credibly? Not sure. That's a challenge.

"I guess I would have to assume that there is no objective definition of beauty. That beauty is not in our genes, it is in our culture.

"I would have to assume, actually, that, therefore, everyone is inherently beautiful. That would be an amazing idea. But I don't know. I guess logically it holds up because who is deciding, anyway? We learn beauty, don't we? That is worth considering.

"Yes, thinking about it that way, what I would credibly have to assume is that everyone is beautiful. That's it."

Often the Thinker's journey toward a credible liberating alternative is instructive in itself. Celia continued, "If you knew that everyone is beautiful, how would you feel about your body?"

Maya smiled for the first time in 20 minutes. "Well," she said, "that would be interesting. I would feel amused, actually. And I would feel passionate about helping other women to know they are beautiful, too. I would feel righteously indignant even, I think, that so many people make so much money injecting us with body hate."

Maya stopped, still smiling.

"And, if you knew that everyone is beautiful," Celia asked again, "how else would you feel about your body?"

"I would feel mostly un-bought-in, released, pleased with the lines and texture of my body. I would feel satisfied to be who I am and to nurture a healthy version of that. I would feel good.

"If I really, really knew that everyone is beautiful, I would feel, actually, detached. Completely detached from that issue. It would be a stranger rather than a strangler.

"I might even laugh."

"And if you knew that everyone is beautiful, how else would you feel about your body?"

"That's all," Maya, said. "Thank you."

"You're welcome," Celia said.

She smiled. "Party?"

CHAPTER 26

What's Wrong With Debate?

Examining The Invitation Question

The Invitation Question is gentle. (It has a long and testy history, but I won't impose that on you here. The fact that I love all of those stories does not mean anyone else will. I am facing this.)

The Invitation Question is a gentle way of saying a not so gentle thing, something like:

> We've got a problem here: your assumption isn't true; but you insist that it is. So, entirely up to you, but don't expect it to get you anywhere. It will never deposit you at your further goal. This time the old maxim is true: you can't get there from here. Not with that assumption. That driver has pulled over, killed the engine and unwrapped a big sandwich.

> However, we will not abandon you to this driver because we are committed to your reaching your further goal. So just describe an acceptable substitute driver, and we'll deliver her to you pronto. You can bring the guy with the sandwich along, too, if you need to. We'll put him in the back seat, and zoom you to your goal. It is not perfect, but sometimes we invoke the progress-not-perfection thing so that we don't make ourselves crazy. This would be one of those times.

This gentle version is:

> Given that the assumption you are making is stopping you
> from reaching your goal, what would you credibly have to
> assume instead in order to reach your goal?

It isn't the path of choice, I know. The best path, as you have seen, is the one that opens up because *you* see that the untrue assumption is untrue. This usually happens during the moments after the question, "Do you think it is true that...?"

Those are moments of facing, and re-thinking and discovery. And following the discovery, you see the world differently. Then you find the true liberating alternative assumption. Taking its place in an Incisive Question, your liberating assumption reveals new terrain and sky and architecture. That's the best.

But when instead you hold on to the untrue limiting assumption as true, we help you locate a credible liberating alternative rather than beating you up to convince you that your assumption is untrue. Your untrue assumption, whether you see it as untrue or not, will continue to block you from your goal until you replace it with a credible liberating one.

Celia did this with Maya. She said:

> Given that the assumption that *there is an inherent*
> *standard of beauty* is stopping you from *feeling happy*
> *about your body*, what would you credibly have to
> assume in order to feel happy about your body?

And note the word *credibly* in this question. It is incredibly important. You have to see the liberating alternative assumption as true enough to consider it. Its credibility carries you to your goal with some conviction – enough, at least, to open your eyes.

What is good about that development is that the Thinking Partner did not drag you there. You got there on your own terms and at your own pace. And that is soon enough. Arriving intact a bit later is better than arriving in harness earlier.

But, you may be wondering, can't the Thinking Partner and I just have a good old-fashioned debate about the Criteria's view of my limiting assumption? Yes, if the Thinker requests it. But probably not as an imposition by the Partner. The lively history of this Invitation Question contains an era of debate between the Thinker and the Thinking Partner about the truth or not of the assumption. And in too many cases the Thinker came out bloody, infantilized and not at all convinced that their assumption was untrue, anyway. And the session stacked up a list of needed repairs.

Once in a while the discussion has been good. But only by negotiation with the Thinker. Otherwise, the Thinker-focus of the Thinking Session shifts to Partner-focus, and the Thinker disengages from their own commitment to the goal.

And that's all I will say about this question's history, promise.

So that's it – the Invitation Question, inviting you as the Thinker to come up with a credible liberating assumption in order to get you to your goal. Even when you and the Criteria disagree.

What you do with the bits of lettuce and the snoring guy in the back seat is up to you.

CHAPTER 27

How Would You Feel?

Examining The Feeling Goal

An important thing about the Feeling Goal: Feelings can come from thinking, from assumptions.

So, unless our hormones are off the chart, or we are drugged, to feel a certain way we need, ironically, to think a certain way. We need to find, eject and replace the untrue cognitive assumption that is making us *feel* bad with the true liberating one that will make us *feel* good.

You can even watch the physiological features of feelings shift in front of you when you ask the Thinker the Incisive Question that contains their true liberating assumption.

So when you feel bad, and you want to feel good, talk with some-one about it first, and cry if you need to. But then try this sequence of questions:

> What am I assuming that is stopping me from feeling good?
>
> (What else am I assuming, etc)
>
> What am I assuming that is *most* stopping me from feeling good?
>
> Do I *think* that assumption is true?
>
> If it is not, what is true and liberating?
>
> If I knew what is true and liberating, how would I feel?

And of course, if you and the Criteria found the key assumption to be true, use the Transition Question to find the untrue one.

And if you and the Criteria just cannot agree about the untrue limiting one, use the Invitation Question to find the true liberating one anyway.

Maya did that, and it worked beautifully. And she experienced that in the session, feeling not only happy about her body, which was her stated goal, but also a range of other good things:

Pleased

Passionate

Amused

Righteously indignant

Calm

Good

Satisfied

Un-bought-in

Released

Celebratory

And all of those showed up on her face and in her eyes, and no doubt, in the temperature and moisture of her skin.

Which, by the way, is why the Incisive Question for a Feeling Goal ends in, "How would you feel about...?" Rather than, as in Maya's goal, "How would you feel *good* about...?"

For one thing, "How would you feel good?" is a weird question. And for another, Maya's mind generated a number of compatible related feelings that enhanced the good feeling. With a Feeling Goal, more is better.

Once again, we are no longer victims. Thinking a certain way can lead to feeling a certain way. Bad feelings are mostly untrue assumptions flapping around under the eaves. We need to notice them, feel them and then change the thinking behind them. And then feel better.

We did not evolve our amazing cortex only to do algebra.

CHAPTER 28

What Is This?

In Practice: The Removing-The-Blocks Goal

It was a leadership workshop in Florida. My niece, Kim, and her friend, Gretchen, were practising the Thinking Session. Gretchen was the Thinker. They called me over.

"What is this?" they asked almost in unison, their noses wrinkling. You would have thought they had found a dried-up frog's thigh under the dinner table.

Kim said, "Gretchen's Further Goal is: I want to remove the blocks to my power. What kind of goal that?"

I love these moments. They are the best of the be-happy-to-be-wrong-in-order-to-get-closer-to-being-right times. And they keep us tuned in to the "anaerobic bacteria and no-music" thing.

And they hurl us back to the question we should be asking all along anyway: what does the Thinker need now in order to keep thinking for herself? That is a much better question than: what is the next question in the sequence?

So, I wondered, what did Gretchen need in order to get rid of the blocks to her power? We unpacked it. Blocks are nearly always untrue limiting assumptions. And there is nearly always one key one. So, Gretchen was in effect asking to find and remove the key untrue limiting assumption that was the block to her power.

So we went through the assumption process and found that her key assumption was: Blondes have no brains. We were getting somewhere.

But what exactly is it that *removes* the block, the limiting assumption?

Is it just finding it? Or do you have to find the true liberating one also? And is that enough? Or do you then need to put it into an Incisive Question?

We went first for the true liberating assumption. Gretchen's was: I have brains to die for.

I wasn't sure then whether that was a sufficient removing of the block. I'm still not completely sure. But our experience so far suggests that it takes more than finding the limiting one and more than finding the liberating one. It takes presenting the liberating one so that it can change the person's view. And that usually takes an Incisive Question.

Otherwise, the liberating assumption just bobs along, bumping against the old limiting assumption that is still head of the department of landscapes.

So we decided to construct an Incisive Question. But suddenly that was a stumper. How would the Incisive Question end? There were tautological whiffs here: If we remove the block by injecting it into an Incisive Question, how do we finish the Question without hooking back into the block? You can't just ask, "If you knew..., how would you remove the blocks to your power?" because the blocks will be removed by the question itself.

By this time Gretchen and Kim probably wished it *had* been a frog's thigh. But they were hanging in there, and we decided to end the question with Gretchen's implied larger goal, which was to express her power. So, having replaced the block – the limiting assumption that blondes have no brains – with "I have brains to die for", we asked, "If you knew that you have brains to die for, how would you express your power?"

It worked. Gretchen thought of seven ways she would express her power, one of which was to tell her friends that our blocks are untrue assumptions, and to get busy.

The next year Removing-The-Blocks appeared on the list of types of Further Goals. It was the seventh. I put it there not because it had won its place by proving its prevalence. But because I thought people should be alerted to it in case it showed up again, and they wouldn't have to pick it up by its tendon.

But those people turned out to be me. Five years went by. This time it was a Coaching Master Class in Britain. 45 people were constructing Incisive Questions on paper with my doing spot demonstrations as we went along. All was hunky dory. Then a young woman said, "I don't know what to do. My goal is to get rid of my limiting beliefs. And when I ask the assumption question, it doesn't get me anywhere."

"That's fine," I said, my good reputation slotted tongue in groove with my 59-year-old confidence, aka arrogance, "but what is your goal?"

She looked puzzled. "Well, it is to get rid of my limiting beliefs."

"Yes," I said again, consciously cultivating Ease, "but what is your further session goal?"

"Well, that's it. At least I thought that's what it was: to get rid of my limiting beliefs."

"Yes, you are right that limiting beliefs, which we call assumptions, will be stopping you from your goal, but what is your goal?" I asked as calmly as I had ever said anything in my whole life.

She now looked stricken. And she studied her paper, completely silent. I stayed attentive, but felt slightly queasy. I was on my bike tilting toward the ravine. But I smiled.

"I don't know now," she whispered. "I thought it was that I want to get rid of my limiting beliefs. But maybe I am wrong. Do I have the wrong goal?" she asked me.

Bike on top of me now, wheel spinning,

"I am sorry, Eugenie; no, your goal is perfect, but could we explore this together in more depth later? I would like to think about it with you."

She said sure and smiled. I smiled back, completely lost.

I went on with the rest of the group, worried they were lost, too, but counting on their assuming it was them, not me. That's not pretty, I know, but getting out of the ravine takes whatever it takes.

We finished the group exercise with lots of successes. And at the end, Eugenie said. "Don't worry about it, Nancy, I think I got it. Thanks." I nodded, relieved. And more confused than ever.

Then, on the M1 going back to London, it hit me. That was a Removing-The-Blocks Goal! One chance in five years, and I had missed it.

I thought it through for 72 miles. And even then I still did not know how we would have ended the Incisive Question because the goal was so different. I reached London before I reached closure on that, and life took over.

Then three years later, Nick, a participant on another course, said, "What I want from this session is to stop believing that I am not working hard enough."

I didn't miss it that time.

It sounds different but it is just the same as Gretchen's and Eugenie's Further Goals. Stopping believing something is the same as getting rid of limiting beliefs, which is the same as removing the blocks.

We just need to remember that blocks and beliefs are limiting assumptions, and that Incisive Questions get rid of them.

I wonder what the next quirky wording of the Removing-The-Blocks Goal will be. Probably something like: "I want to incinerate the dead body parts of my perceptions."

But we will be ready.

CHAPTER 29

How Do You Live Without It?

When The Incisive Question Is Off Limits

Such good things emerge from the Incisive Question that if you are not careful, it can become an end in itself. Some people find themselves feeling that the Session has fallen short of perfection if it has not led to the explicit construction of an Incisive Question.

But sometimes an explicit Incisive Question is the wrong thing.

Sometimes, as we have seen, Part I is plenty. It does the job, and the Thinker is finished.

Sometimes also the Thinker wants to *understand why* they feel or do things. Sometimes they want just to *look at their assumptions*. Sometimes they want to explore a *new topic* altogether. Sometimes they need to get *information* about their topic before they go further. Sometimes they want to do an *activity* in the session in addition to talking about it.

And, unless they get stuck, they do not need Incisive Questions to achieve any of those Further Goals. The last three of the goals, in fact, don't even need Part III, the working through assumptions, either.

But if you start to have withdrawal symptoms from the pleasure of seeing the impact of Incisive Questions, enjoy this fact: *implicit* Incisive Questions are occurring all the time. The most important ones are the ones that your Attention and the other Components and your warmth and trust in the Thinker are asking every second. Questions like:

> If you knew that you are intelligent, what more would
> you think?

If you knew that I welcome whatever you need to say, what would you feel?

If you knew that your thinking matters, what other ideas would occur to you?

If you knew that I am interested, where would your thinking take you next?

And so you can, once again, relax. The Thinker will go where they need most to go. And that may not be down an explicit Incisive Question path. If you insist on taking them there anyway, you will have to back up and apologize. Taking them where they have not asked to go, taking them down your route, however starry its sky, infantilizes them. And they stop thinking.

So it is easier just to read the signals that are right there inside their answer to the Part II Question (what more do you want to achieve in this session?). Listen for *their* Further Goal. If it tells you they don't need Incisive Questions, it will also tell you what they do need.

Delivering that is where the real pleasure is anyway.

CHAPTER 30

Why Do I Do This?

In Practice: The Understanding-Why-I Goal

Guilt is not genetic, but sometimes you wonder. It is so findable in the human being, you'd think it came with the package.

But truly it doesn't. It comes, I agree, with things human beings construct. Most religions, for example, would fall apart without guilt. And so would schools. And most organizations. And even a lot of marriages.

So it is not the easiest thing in yourself to challenge, even when it is eating your life alive.

Of course I am not talking about situational guilt, the kind you feel when you actually do something wrong. If you pocket the community tips, guilt would be warranted, and might make you put it all back. If you yell when you could just as well say the thing with some warmth, guilt can lead you to apologize, soften your voice, and send a rose. Guilt like that has a purpose.

The guilt I am talking about is the deep-down-I-am-a-bad-person kind of guilt that moves like superglue from one part of you to another, and dries.

That kind of guilt ruins lives. It comes from untrue limiting assumptions of the deepest order. And most of us imagine catastrophic levels of collapse of the things it holds together when we even think about exploring it. And we don't know why we feel it. We don't know that untrue assumptions power guilt.

Hala said, "I want to understand why I feel guilty all of the time." (This Understanding-Why-I goal is a good match for guilt.)

"What are you assuming," I asked her, "that is making you feel guilty all of the time?"

"I am assuming that I am bad. I am assuming that I am not as good as my brother. I am assuming that no matter what I do, it is not enough."

"And what else are you assuming that is making you feel guilty all of the time?"

"That when God forgives, he leaves a little left over that he doesn't forgive."

"What else are you assuming that is making you feel guilty all of the time?"

"That I cannot ever do enough. That's all. I feel kind of sick."

Guilt can make anyone feel sick. I'll bet that guilt will show up one day as one of the top five suppressors of the human immune system.

But she wasn't throwing up yet. So I asked her the question that would identify the key limiting assumption, which would be her answer to why.

"Of those assumptions, or any that might spring to mind, what is the one most making you feel guilty all of the time?"

"That I can never do enough."

I memorized it.

Then she said, "No, that's not it. It is that whatever good things I do, however impressive or heartfelt, don't count after a day."

I memorized that one, wishing it had been shorter, but deciding to look heroic.

Then she said, "Actually, no, that's not it either. I am assuming that I am only as good as the sum total of my deeds."

I didn't have to memorize that one. I knew it well.

I checked, though, "Your key assumption is that you are only as good as the sum total of your deeds?"

"Yes, that's it."

"And," I went on, "do you think it is true that you are only as good as the sum total of your deeds?"

"Yes," she said without drawing breath. "I know it is true."

"Know?" I thought. "This should be interesting." The Philosophical Choice had already made confetti out of that assumption. And I could not imagine what information or logic Hala could round up to make a convincing case.

"What are your reasons for thinking it is true that you are only as good as the sum total of your deeds?" I asked her, truly curious.

"It is true that I am the sum total of my deeds because Jesus said so. At least I think he did. No, maybe he didn't. Anyway, my minister says so. And that's good enough.

"Also, if we didn't think that we are the sum total of our deeds, we probably would just become slobs, and then where would the world be? And besides all of that, it is in doing, not being, that we find our purpose. If I stopped doing deeds, life would be pointless."

She looked at me.

"Any more reasons you think it is true that you are only as good as the sum total of your deeds?"

"Yes, my father made that very clear to me, and I really loved my father."

"Hmm," I thought, "not too good in Three Criteria department. No information or logic here, and not aligned with the Positive Philosophical Choice which would say that we are good and of value inherently, just because we *are*, not because of what we *do*.

"She's found the untrue assumption but thinks it is true," I thought. "Not ideal. But at least the Invitation Question will help."

But something was happening. She took a deep breath. She started to cry.

"You know," she said, "that's all boloney. Isn't it? I mean, nothing I just said actually proves that only our deeds make us good. Just because people I love or admire say things doesn't make them true per se, right?

"So," she breathed again and blew her nose, "your question was, do *I* think it is true that I am only as good as the sum total of my deeds? Do

I?" She looked out across the room. "Do I? Now that is an interesting question. I have never ever thought about this for myself."

She was quiet for a minute, at least.

"I would never tell my daughters that they are only as good as the sum total of their deeds. I knew the minute they were born, each of them, that they were good deep down right that minute, a holy kind of good. God was in them. Nothing else mattered.

"Maybe the same would have to be true of me, too. I wonder.

"So, no, Nancy. No, maybe it is not true. Maybe it is not true at all," she said. "Logically, factually as far as anyone knows, and definitely philosophically, the assumption is not true."

This was an Understanding-Why-I Goal. She now understood why she felt guilty all of the time. She wanted to understand, not to change, the feeling. So, that was that.

Except for a kind of drawing together question, "Are you satisfied that you have reached your goal of understanding why you feel guilty all of the time?"

"Yes," she said. "Definitely. And I am also just plain satisfied. With me. With my existence. For the moment, at least. And that is a first."

What she needed now was to leave that goal as achieved and have a chance to decide what she wanted next. So I asked her, "What more would you like to achieve in this session?"

"Nothing today," she said. "I need to let this settle in. Part of me would like to get rid of the assumption. But I already feel changed. A bit like my garden after a storm. I can pick up the branches later. I now just want to look at the sky."

CHAPTER 31

Why Not?

Examining The Understanding-Why-I Goal

When people want to understand why they think, feel or do something, that is all they want. It is a lot. It can change their life. So when they have found out "why," stop. Don't push them.

The key reason people think, feel or do things that they don't want to think, feel or do is usually an untrue limiting assumption. They need to find it. That's all. They can find it with a trip through most, but not all, of Part III of the Session. They find it, and they stop, just before looking for the true liberating assumption. Let them. They are there.

How do you know for sure that they are there?

They say so. They say in Part II that they want to understand why they... Or they might have worded it as, "I want to figure out what is making me..." or some other variant that definitely is a request to understand "why" about themselves. (However, if their question is something like: "I want to understand why the universe is expanding," that is different. That is an "Information" goal. No amount of unearthing assumptions is going to help them understand the universe. "Understanding why I" is very different from "understanding why". These tiny words like "I" are killers if you ignore them.)

So, once they have found the untrue limiting assumption, they are home. Don't lead them blindly toward a liberating assumption and then to an Incisive Question. (You won't have a goal to hook the liberating assumption to when you get there, anyway, and you will just have to double back. So you might as well keep this important feature of the

Understanding-Why-I-Goal in mind and avoid the traffic jam.)

A lot of us see action as the only road to change. And that near fanaticism can creep into Thinking Sessions. So we need to watch it. We need to let "understanding why" about oneself be enough.

If it isn't, the Thinker will tell us. They will tell us they want to go on. And Incisive Questions will be perfect. But not until then.

We lost some clients not understanding this. But you will have to read the first book to find out about that fiasco. Another blunder that led us finally to the music.

CHAPTER 32

What Are They All?

In Practice: The Looking-At-Assumptions Goal

As you can see, assumptions rule. So you may occasionally want to look at them. Just look. Nothing more. Flush them out and see what you have been putting up with all this time. There is relief in that in a funny sort of way. Analysis often offers relief.

Here is how Ling experienced it:

"What I want more from this session," he told Maria, "is to look at my assumptions around this issue."

Ling had been exploring the radical idea of getting organized. "It just makes sense," he had said, "that if I get organized, I will accomplish more and know where I am with everything. But it would be a first. And if my mother heard this, and she weren't dead, she would die. Anyway, that's what I want from the rest of the session."

Maria smiled, "What are you assuming that is stopping you from getting organized?"

"I am assuming I was born this way. I am assuming there are unique manifestations of God, and this is one of them. I am assuming being disorganized is an art form. I am assuming that to be organised is a negative thing. And that I will let people down because they will then *expect* me to be organized, and I won't be able to keep it up."

"See what I mean?" Ling smiled.

"And what else are you assuming," Maria continued, "that is stopping you from getting organized?"

"Well, that I won't be me any more. That I am genetically incapable of walking into a room and leaving it organized. That you can be only one thing or the other, so to be organized I will have to be completely organized every minute."

He stopped. "I think that is all."

Knowing there could be more assumptions and that only Ling could know for sure, Maria asked again, "And what else might you be assuming that is stopping you from getting organized?"

"Interesting, I am assuming that my whole life would be about being absolutely organized every second; that if I am organized, I will never do anything else."

"And what else are you assuming," Maria, asked, "that is stopping you from getting organized?"

"That it would be a surrender to all of the people, like my mother, who have nagged at me about this for years. That I would in that way be conforming. That I would become a pawn. That I would become boring and predictable.

"Amazing. Where do these live? That's it, though," he said.

Remembering that Ling's Further Goal was just to *look at all of the assumptions*, not to do anything with them, Maria simply asked, "Then are you satisfied that you have looked at all of the assumptions around this issue?"

"I think so," Ling said. "And I am surprised at some of them. That I can't be myself and be organized for example. The thought that I might not be the disorganization in my life is pretty amazing."

So Maria returned to Part II. "What more would you like to achieve from the rest of this session?"

"Nothing." Ling said. "I got what I needed. It is a help just to know what these little monsters are.

"In an organized sort of way," he said.

CHAPTER 33

Who Is In Charge Here?

Examining The Looking-At-Assumptions Goal

How easy was that?

Assumptions are most dangerous when they remain in our unconscious. So just to know what assumptions are there can be a relief. They are stupid. Some of them are silly. Some are ugly. But they are finite. Once we dig them all out of the cellar, we see how relatively few there are. And exposed to sun they shrivel some.

If they stick to the patio, we can come back and power-hose them. Incisive Questions are good at that.

CHAPTER 34

Not Even Assumptions?

In Practice: New-Topic, Information, Activity Goals

We have found three Further Goals that do not go even to Part III. No assumptions. No Incisive Questions. But powerful just the same.

They are really simple to navigate. Here they are:

New-Topic Goal

Nathan was thinking about how to get to the gym every morning. He figured that out. Then in answer to Part II he said he wanted to think about getting a wonderful camera. He did that, too. Then in answer to another Part II he said he wanted to figure out how best to negotiate his new contract. He did it. Then he was finished and went home, thrilled. He didn't need once to explore assumptions. He just needed to think and talk and think. The first topic. Then a new topic. Then another one. All Incisive Questions *implicitly asked* by the mind itself in Part I.

No Part III.

Information Goal

Let's say the Thinker is thinking along and suddenly they need facts or figures or an update. You can help them find those things. Maybe you even have them yourself. But maybe not and they need Google. Or a colleague. Or a printout. Or a little more life experience.

What they don't need is a trawl through assumptions or an Incisive Question.

Information only. No Part III.

Activity Goal

And sometimes the Thinker needs to *do* something. Right there in the session. This is different from an Action Goal, which you will remember is usually not a request to *do* anything. It is a more subdued kind of action, like deciding, figuring out how, making a plan... I wish those two words were not so much alike, but they are.

Anyway, in an Activity Goal the Thinker actually *does* things like: write the speech, craft the announcement, make the phone call, practise the presentation, role-play the dialogue, fill out the form, compose the song, pray, try the recipe. And the Thinker wants you there, providing a Thinking Environment for them while they do it.

Sometimes they will get stuck and, at their request, you can ask them what they are assuming and find an Incisive Question to free them. But most Activity Goals are just doing the thing.

One important other thing about this Goal: It is not an opportunity for you to crank up your Blackberry and get to work on your email while the Thinker does whatever their activity is. This is their session. It may not look like thinking, but it is. And they will need your Attention in order to do it superbly.

These three types of further Goals, with no explicit work on assumptions, are perfect, and we need to let them be just that. There will be other days for Incisive Questions.

CHAPTER 35

When Can I Write It Down?

In Practice: Part V, Recording The Incisive Question

"You mean I can't take notes any more?"

You would have thought I had said that chocolate was over. I was speaking to a conference of counsellors. I was asked nine questions. Five of them were about taking notes. They just couldn't get it: note-taking compromises Attention.

That doesn't mean you can't *ever* take notes again. Sometimes you have to, really, really have to. But most of the time you just think you have to. Because you have been doing it for years and because you haven't actually started listening in this way. The kind of listening that ignites the human mind – and this is a perk of this work – helps you remember things. Real listening also means you don't miss anything. The minute you take a note, you miss something, you are behind. The Thinker is off and you are running after them, waving your pen to get them to slow down. And that of course means that the Attention you do have for them is no longer generative.

They wonder what you are writing. They wonder why you are writing. You, subtly, have become the focus of the session. Your notes have, actually. They are determining where your Attention goes next.

I think we have to face this. Note-taking is rarely a Thinking Environment. And you can make time at the end of the session, when they are gone, to make the notes you think you will need.

And if you have to fill in forms with the person, well, get it over with as soon as possible. And begin to re-think what else, other than the forms, might work better anyway.

If they, on the other hand, want to take notes, that is a different ball game. Many people do think well, best sometimes, on paper. And with your Attention and their pen or keyboard, they can have a superb session.

Similarly, if you and they are having a conversation in answer to Part II, and part of what you want to convey requires you to draw or write, that works.

And, of course, if the Thinker asks you to write, write. That works.

Notes are one official part of the Session sequence, actually. Just before the Session ends, the Thinker needs to write down their Incisive Question. The Incisive Question can be elusive for a while. After all, it is defying years of co-habitation with the untrue assumption. Writing the Incisive Question down captures it in exactly the words the Thinker used to create it. So we help them preserve the Question by asking them to write it down.

Then, we ask them if they want to write anything else from the session. Often they do. We give them Attention while they do. Attention from beginning to end keeps them thinking well.

The Thinker's notes are one thing. That works fine. It is note-taking in the session by the partner or counsellor or advisor or coach, for their own purposes, that doesn't work so well. Not well enough.

Not for unleashing the human mind.

CHAPTER 36

What Do You Respect?

In Practice: Part VI – Appreciation

At the very end we appreciate each other. We think better between sessions if we do.

This is different from thanking each other. That's good, too. But appreciation that keeps people thinking well seems to be a simple offering of admiration, of respect. And, as we saw in the chapter on Appreciation, it works best when it is sincere, succinct and specific. And let your words take you beyond the session. Find a quality you have noticed in them in other situations, too. It will mean more. This is not feedback on the session. It is an observation of them.

What is a quality you admire in that person? That's all. Say it. Leave it. Let it sink in.

And then they will appreciate you back.

And when you receive it, say, "Thank you." Don't question or rebuff it. It is their gift to you.

It is their *thinking*.

CHAPTER 37

Is There A Difference?

Assumption vs Belief

Some things come to light slowly. In one of those amazing baths, this one in Rancho Santa Fe, California, and in the very early years of understanding the Thinking Environment, I was pondering the beauty of The Incisive Question for liberating thinking. I had not at that time fully understood why it worked so brilliantly, nor how dependably to replicate that brilliance.

Clearly The Incisive Question got rid of the block to thinking. Every time. But what exactly was the block? Session after session danced across my mind like Sugarplums. (It was Christmas.) And bingo, I realized the obvious. The block to good thinking is an assumption. An assumption. So simple. As usual.

Good bath.

But why not a belief? It did not occur to me that the block to thinking would be a belief. The word never came up for review. Assumption was it. And I was ignorant then about other thinking methodologies that use the word "belief" to describe blocks in people's lives. So I used the word assumption from then on, and it has been a powerhouse.

But over the years I have taught many people who have studied other methodologies and say "limiting belief" and "self-limiting belief". And they have begun to ask me about the choice of the world "assumption". I think their question is interesting.

I also think it matters, the way getting the right transportation matters when your destination matters. It is pretty tough to get to Ft Worth from

San Francisco if you travel by pogo stick. From the shape you'd be in when you arrived, there would be nothing Ft Worth could do to make it worth your journey. Not even the old videos of Will Rogers.

Here's the point. Both assumption and belief are words for perception. I perceive myself to be inferior, for example, and so I assume I am, or I believe I am. The two words express the same perception, but they build very *different relationships with me*.

The word "belief" builds a relationship of surrender or faith. The word "assumption" builds a relationship of question, responsibility and change. When I say "assumption," I immediately question the perception. When I say "belief," I accept it. When we use the word "belief", the perception is in charge of us. Using the word "assumption", we are in charge of the perception.

Now that *relationship* with the word, when it comes to freeing our thinking and our lives, becomes crucial. If we are truly to take charge of our lives, we need to use language that lets us do that. The minute I say, "my assumption is that I am inferior," I am saying – because of the very definition of assumption – it might not be true.

"Belief," on the other hand, says, "This perception is beyond examination. I am surrendered to it. It is fixed." Using the word "belief," we have to work harder to see that we have choice about that perception. The word "belief" keeps us, subtly, in its grip.

So the question, "What are you assuming that is holding you back from your goal," for example, will send perceptions to your mind that already you are questioning, and about which you see instantaneously you have choice. "What belief do you have that is holding you back from your goals," on the other hand, will send perceptions to your mind that you do not question instantaneously.

(I think there is a place for the word "belief" in our lives. Just as there is a place for faith. But the whole point of faith, when it really gets going and makes a positive difference, is that it is not a state of speculation. It is an acceptance. It is a decision not to question. It is a kind of surrender. And this kind of surrender is, paradoxically, a particular act of being in charge.)

Concepts and conviction arise in large part because of the language we use to get us there. If your goal is release from perceptions that are victimizing you, if your goal is to take charge of your life and change it for the better, you will want to consider using a vehicle that is itself not victimizing, and that goes fast with entirely renewable fuel. The word "assumption" is just that vehicle.

Language matters. We live it and in it. Most importantly, we *think* in it. A question I have continued to ask myself throughout these years, and still do in every session, is: What words will free the human mind in front of me? The distinction between the word "assumption" and the word "belief" is just one of many precise choices of words that seem to be essential if truly independent, fresh thinking is our destination.

I think this, even though I was the pogo stick champion of Clovis.

CHAPTER 38

How Else?

Introducing The Other Applications

The Thinking Partnership is one application of the Ten Components of a Thinking Environment. It produces the most independent thinking from the Thinker. It is the most generative.

If there were such thing as purity, the Thinking Partnership process would be one version. It comes as close as anything we know to reproducing what the human mind does naturally when it moves like lightning.

So, let's leave it there. Shimmering.

The other Applications are stars as well. The next pages share five more applications for pairs. Then four for groups.

I think that if The Ten Components became the culture of our coaching, our coach supervision, our mentoring, our conversations and dialogue, our defusing of conflict, our meetings, our facilitation, our public speaking and our gathering of wisdom, we would most days stretch out on the grass with our hands behind our head, amazed.

So let's see what can happen in pairs.

CHAPTER 39

Why Would You Ever Do Anything Else?

Coaching In A Thinking Environment

Your client arrives. You smile. You say hello. You settle in.

Then what do you do?

Better question: Then what do you assume?

What you assume in that moment determines the entire path of the session, and its success.

Some coaches assume that they are the architects of the session. They assume that there is only one expert in the room, and that they are it. Some coaches arrive with an invisible kit of tools to take the client to wherever they assess the client should go. They assume that their job is to think for the client.

But maybe you are an exception. Maybe you assume, instead, that in front of you is a formidable mind. Maybe you assume that your expertise is not to direct that mind, but to free it.

Maybe you know that the point of a coaching session is the client's thinking – figuring things out, looking into the long grass, conceiving, pondering, accessing hinterland, facing, seeing, deciding, riding an oxalis cloud – being themselves and planning from there.

Maybe you really, really mean it when you repeat the coach's "mantra" that the client can generate the best answers to their own questions.

Maybe, as you smile and say hello and settle in, you can hardly wait to find what ideas the client will conceive that only they can, and you cannot. Maybe you have set down quietly all of your agile interventions and are happy if the client never needs them. Maybe you are about to be so present, you will become invisible.

Maybe your humility in front of this pulsating intelligence resounds.

Maybe you suspect that as coaching comes into its own, our focus should be profoundly on the client, that our focus should be profoundly not on ourselves.

Maybe you suspect also that the key responsibility of the coach is to halt the epidemic of obedience and the unwitting development of the sophisticated victim in our clients, especially our executive clients.

Maybe you know that it is not the coach, but the client, whose time has come.

I hope so. If so, the best will be born and you will be there, once again to be in awe. And at the end, you will know the joy of carrying your client to their own answers, and yourself to the mystery of mattering profoundly because you do not matter at all. It is inside paradox that you do your best work.

So, let's imagine that the point of coaching is to generate the client's best thinking (still a radical idea apparently). I think it takes two things to do this. It takes 1) the building of relationship in a Thinking Environment, and 2) the mastery of the Thinking Session Sequence of Questions that replaces blocks with breakthroughs (untrue limiting assumptions with true liberating ones).

Could we consider that a coach's first responsibility, then, may be to develop their own expertise in the Ten Components and in the Thinking Session Sequence of Questions? With that expertise in place, a coach can then offer any other response, process, model, framework or diagnostic. The Thinking Environment adds quality and client-autonomy to all coaching conversations. I think it may be essential infrastructure.

Coaches can then ask themselves, "Am I, in what I am doing in this moment, ensuring the independent thinking of my client? If not, what do I need to do to revive it?" As Linda Aspey said, "You have to value the client's thinking more than you value your own."

The Coaching Relationship

Let's look first at the thing that matters most: the building of relationship. Ernesto Spinelli and Eric de Haan assert that the value of coaching lies most of all in the *client's* experience of the relationship with the coach. If the coach thinks the relationship is good, but the client doesn't, it isn't. And the value of the coaching experience erodes.

Building relationship is complex. Some of it is ineffable, defying instruction or analysis. But when you take apart the highest quality coaching relationships, you find the Ten Components of a Thinking Environment. It is these ten behaviours, as Stephanie Archer said, that are the key relational aspect of successful coaching. The Ten Components come first. They guide the interaction. They become the culture. The relationship thrives. Once the coach has established these ten behaviours as the relational norm, coaching at its best becomes possible.

The Sequence Of Questions

You could say that Thinking Environment Coaching lies on a spectrum – from more independent thinking by the client at one end, to more direction by the coach at the other. And even at the coach-directive end, if the Ten Components stay intact, there is greater independent thinking by the client than there can be without them.

Let's say that as coach you are committed to the client's independent thinking and, therefore, to creating and sustaining a Thinking Environment throughout. You know that the client needs first to generate all of their own thinking and that you, therefore, start with Part I of this Sequence of Questions. You are prepared for that to be enough. Just two questions: "What would you like to think about, and what are your thoughts?" and, "What more do you think, or feel or want to say?"

This is for some coaches a huge challenge. I once watched a coach try hard at this, and fail within the first 90 seconds. Bob began well. He said with just the right pacing and warmth, "What would you like to think about in our session? And what are your thoughts?"

"I want to figure out the best way to succeed," Alice said. "I want to be strategic this time. But I also want to focus on my happiness and health.

"I remember how in school praise motivated me, but how empty I felt with all those A's and no idea of who I was. And I have a philosophy about money that is both empowering and debilitating." She paused.

"Also, I am not sure whether to stay in my apartment or move." She was quiet. She was still thinking.

But Bob blew it. He spoke. "Now, getting back to your main goal," he said, "what will your success look like a year from now, say?"

I stopped the session. "What led you to ask her that, Bob?"

"She was all over the place," he said. "She was not focused."

"What were the indications that she was not focused?" I asked him.

"Seven topics in a row? I'd say that lacked focus, wouldn't you?"

"But they seem like strands of the same topic to me," Alice said. "And I can't get strategic about success until I can consider all of the strands."

"So," I said, "if you were to trust that Alice in each word *is* focusing on her goal, what would you do?"

"Yeah, okay," he said. "I'd just relax, I guess, and do nothing."

"I agree that you would relax," I said, "But you would never do nothing. Your Attention and your interest are exact opposites of nothing. They are the reason she will reach her goal."

Bob agreed to try it. It worked. Alice was pleased with the results. But Bob remained anxious. He grew relaxed over time. But the transition was hard for him.

Why? Because for us as coaches to become a catalyst for superb independent thinking in a client, there has to be eruption. It is as if we have to disgorge and rearrange all of the organs of our expertise. They fall out on the table. And nothing goes back in quite the same order.

Our urges have to change. We have to give up the pull to do *for* the client. We have to cultivate a need to discover their process, their ideas, their words, their way.

We have been walking in boots. Now we must pirouette across the wire.

We must look through the kaleidoscope from the other end.

We must jerk ourselves away from the copse, and run to the cliff edge.

We must stop knowing, and start wondering.

We must coach, not control.

So, let's say the client has generated all of the thinking they can. Part I is over. They need now to determine for themselves whether the *session* is over. You don't decide this for them. You move to Part II and ask the client what more they want to achieve in the session.

If they need information, you supply it or support them to get it. If they want to think about a new topic, you construct a new Part I and ask them a question tailored for that topic. If they want to achieve something related to, but not quite accomplished in Part I, they probably need to find and replace the untrue limiting assumptions that are in their way. So you offer them Parts III and IV of the Sequence of Questions, navigating with them appropriately. You have seen these pathways of the Session in our previous chapters.

But let's say they ask for something different from these. Let's say they say, "I want your input. I want to know what you see that I don't see. I want to know where you would take me." Or let's say that your coaching agreement with them is that at this point you will always design the next step in the session.

How do you do this? How do you intervene with input or direction or other frameworks or models without even subtly doing the client's thinking for them?

You do it holding onto all Ten Components. And the second you intervene, you keep your Thinking Environment radar sharp because, if you get on a roll and lose track, the client's independent thinking will be the first thing to go, long before you run out of things to offer.

Effective coaching interventions abound. To feast on most of them all in one place I recommend Sunny Stout-Rostron's superb, comprehensive, scholarly and friendly book, *Business Coaching Wisdom And Practice*.

And have the pleasure of seeing team coaching from a refreshing new angle in Helena Dolny's book, *Team Coaching: Artists At Work*.

Then whatever you choose to learn and to use, let the Ten Components permeate it.

You also can create what I call the "Coach's Incisive Question". You create the Incisive Question *for* the client. You remember the content of Part I. You decide what their further session goal should be. You choose their key untrue limiting assumption. You create their liberating alternative assumption. And from that you construct an Incisive Question. Then you ask it. You have a 50 percent chance of being two rings from bulls-eye. Because it is not the client's own construction, it is not a work of genius. But it can work.

You can, in fact, create an Incisive Question lots of places. In any of your observations or input, for example, or any of the other models and methods you use, you can remove untrue limiting assumptions through an Incisive Question. If you do it accurately enough (and that is a challenge), and without a fibre of infantilization (also a challenge), the client's mind may leap. In fact, in every coaching method, when the client's mind leaps, there has probably just been an Incisive Question, spoken or silent.

And, again, if you do keep your radar sharp, you will notice when the client's independent thinking is choking to death; and you can do a Heimlich. The Ten Components nearly always get the client's autonomy breathing again.

Whatever the intervention, it will have value proportionate to your focus on the true goal of independent client thinking – especially if you are willing to abandon the intervention the second you have become the star of the show and the client has become the audience.

Most important, allowing the Thinking Session Sequence of Questions to be your infrastructure, starting point and primary reference point sharpens your judgement about what other processes to use. Without this Sequence your judgement can spring too much from an arbitrary collection of tools.

"But isn't the Sequence of Questions essentially a script?" someone asked me once. "In fact," he said, "if as a client I knew what questions my coach was going to ask me, I probably wouldn't hire them. I could just ask myself those questions."

There are two important issues here. First, the Thinking Session Sequence of Questions is an ever-revealing-itself-to-us representation of what the mind naturally seems to ask itself when it breaks through. It is what the mind seems to want to do. So we learn the up-to-date way to do it. And we offer that catalytic sequence because it is brilliant, and it is experienced as new every time.

And the coach is always thinking second-to-second about what the client needs next in order to keep thinking for themselves well. There is nothing rote here.

Second, asking yourself the questions doesn't work well enough. Something happens for you, something generatively generative, when the questions come from the coach. I suspect that the coach's Attention and skill are silently removing other deep untrue limiting assumptions you have about yourself. Certainly something makes it powerful. We will no doubt understand this one day. But we can rely on it today.

"And what about all of that repeating of the very same question? How can that possibly be good coaching?" the same person asked. This is a fascinating phenomenon. Heraclitus comes to mind. He pointed out a while back (400 BCE) that one cannot step into the same river twice. I think something similar is happening here. With every asking, the very same question produces very different results. And the same person who is generating the answers is a different person after each asking.

And so, in a sense, the question, like the river, is not the same at all. Every molecule of the thinker and the issue is different after each asking of the question. And the question is experienced as different by the Thinker each time it is asked. And when the question is no longer generative, we stop asking it. In practice, then, the same question, if it is astutely constructed, is a fresh, crystalline question each time.

A word about what some people consider the three responsibilities of the coach:

Tasking (establishing action steps and accountability

Holding Up the Mirror (getting the client to see things they haven't seen, about themselves or their situation)

And Challenging (getting the client to examine the efficacy of their thinking)

First, all of these things happen naturally in the full Thinking Session: the Incisive Question, unless it is for a Feeling Goal, nearly always leads to action steps; and at the end of the session, the client determines what kind of accountability works best for them.

Second, Part III of the Session (the work on assumptions) "holds up the mirror" most directly and productively for the client. It does so in such a way that the client is able to think for themselves well about what they then see in "the mirror."

Part III is, as you have seen, an experience of profound challenge for the client. But because the challenge is their choice and their path, the results are truly theirs. Also, autonomy is usually more challenging than autocracy.

So becoming expert at the Sequence of Questions seems to me essential in coaching.

But even some Thinking Environment skill in coaching is better than none. In fact, if suddenly the world of coaching were to be populated with coaches who knew how to be present, still, engaged, connected through ease and profound respect for, and trust in, the client's intelligence, interested in what the client will say and think next, and if these Coaches would decide absolutely never ever, ever to interrupt their client from this day forward amen, the quality of Coaching in the world would shoot up overnight, faster than corn in Iowa.

But, ah, if you know the Thinking Environment intimately and your Attention is generative, like sun, you might get something like this:

"I would like to think about Ned," said Jim, a CEO in a biotech firm. "He is a brilliant strategist. He is one of the best brains in the business. Also, he is a compelling, dynamic speaker. He is indefatigable. And he can be charming."

Jim paused.

"But I think he is slowly destroying the emotional fabric of my senior team. His non-people-related work is superb. Yet, something sinister seems to be happening, something beneath the building, as it were. It is as if he is picking apart slowly the very things he has constructed."

Jim stopped. He said, "That's it."

"What more do you think, or feel or want to say?" I asked him, slowly.

He said, "I was reading a biography of Saddam Hussein. The author described Saddam's personality profile. As I read those lines, I thought, 'God, this profile of Saddam fits Ned.' He can savage people who disagree with him. He doesn't consider the consequences of his actions. He 'expunges' people if they are not loyal to him. He seems unable to feel what people are going through; he lacks empathy. And he can indulge in grandiosity.

"The author says that these characteristics make up Narcissistic Personality Disorder."

Jim paused. He looked at me.

He looked away. He was quiet. I listened to his silence.

"After I read that passage, I immediately Googled Narcissistic Personality Disorder. That was chilling. And a week later I went to see the country's expert on narcissism. I told her about Ned.

"Her response was sobering. 'People with NPD make sure that the success of the organization is not sustainable. And therapy is rarely successful with them because the pathology eventually interprets the therapist as inflicting a *narcissistic injury*, and the patient expunges the therapist from their life.'

"I told her that I could see the dangers of Ned's behaviour, but I felt sorry for him because of the emptiness in him.

"The psychologist said, 'You may feel sorry for Ned, but feel sorry at a distance.'"

Jim took a deep breath. He looked at me intensely.

"I can't figure this out," he said. He put his head in his hands and leaned forward. He was quiet.

Then he looked up. "Of course I can figure this out,' he said. "I am not stupid."

Jim looked at me and smiled.

He looked out again and shifted in his seat.

"The trouble is, I would like to share my understanding with the others on my team, in order to think together about his impact on the organization. But that could be dangerous."

He looked down again.

"Actually," he said suddenly, "it doesn't have to be dangerous. I could do it carefully and well.

"But Ned's contract goes for 18 more months.

"I just don't know what will protect my team and the company from Ned's pathology while retaining his strategic talents."

He looked out beyond me, into that productive space of nowhere.

Then he looked at me.

"Actually," he said, "maybe I could make a structural change that would take him out of the people role and keep him in a senior strategy role."

Jim looked down and again was quiet.

"Whatever change I make, though, could make him feel betrayed, and then I would become the injurer," he said. Many seconds passed.

Then he looked at me. He said, "You know, I just had a thought. I could enlist *him* in designing this re-structuring. I could use his very talent so that the structure he creates escapes his destroying it." He paused. "Yes, this could work. I will talk with the others."

Jim looked away again. Then he looked back. His eyes were warm. "Thank you," he said. "Thank you."

"What more would you like from the session?" I asked.

"Nothing," Jim said, "that was perfect."

Or you might get something like this:

"I want to reclaim my own humming," Jake said.

"Interesting," I thought, not used to hearing language like that from an investment banker. I listened.

"My own humming is too small in relation to all the hardness of Wall Street," Jake continued. "I must become the hardness. My humming won't fit in with the hardness. It might move gently around and alter some of the hardness, but really that is not what Wall Street is about. There is no room for stories or poetry. No room for humming.

"Someone will tell me that this is not a good idea. That humming won't do. That being that alive won't do. But I question all that. Trans-acting leaves me no time for my own story. People have forgotten their own stories."

He looked at me. I kept listening.

"I need to find more nourishing places to be with people. But if I let my humming grow, my foundations at work will rock."

He paused. He looked at me. He looked through me. I kept my eyes on his eyes. I saw, but did not know, the progression. He was banking, wings tipped.

"That is stupid," he said. "It is not true. By focusing on my experience, I will lead myself to more of myself. Actually, my survival depends on

185

managing the hardness. I must give myself scope."

He stopped. He said, "My humming has to be very, very quiet."

He paused. He looked at his hands. I wondered what he "saw".

"No," he said, "if I choose, the humming could be very, very loud. It doesn't have to be a little bit on the side."

He frowned. "Maybe the hardness is bigger than my humming," he said.

"No," he said, his brow smoothing. "My humming can influence the people I am with anytime."

He looked right at me. "If I knew," he said, "if I knew, really knew, that my humming can influence the people I am with anytime, I would build no fence around it. And I would watch instead of closing my eyes, instead of leaving."

He tossed his head back and then looked at me. "I can influence them. I can use my position for good in this way. I can start by meeting with Arden tomorrow. 3pm.

"Thank you," he said.

"There will be a difference from this."

I smiled.

Ten minutes. A new direction. A new life? A new leader? Someday a new economics?

And so, I wonder, with the potential for this much beauty, why, unless implored, would you ever do anything else?

CHAPTER 40

What Are We Doing Here?

Contracting As Coach

You are with a potential client. In this conversation you want to establish two things:

1) what your client wants from their experience

2) how you coach.

This may seem obvious, but you would be surprised how many coaches do the first, but not the second. And this is because professionals assume (and this assumption is fathoms deep, and takes a lot of reeling in to flop on the deck) that when what they do is mysterious to the client, the client is impressed. They think that it keeps the client returning again and again to the source of something they could never do themselves. Some coaches even assume that if the client knows exactly what the coach is doing, the client will not pay. So they don't tell them.

This is a big mistake. It turns out that human beings prefer to know than to be in the dark. They prefer to feel powerful than in awe. They return most readily to those professionals who have stopped the David Copperfield thing and told them exactly what they will be doing and why. People, strangely enough, actually like to be equals.

This probably doesn't mean that you want your brain surgeon to tell you about every little slice and probe into all those ganglia. But it does mean, even with brain surgery, that the surgeon tells you lots about what she will be doing. And when it comes to coaching, the client does want to know what is happening to the ganglia and lobes. They want to know as precisely as possible what the coach is doing. It allows them to think clearly and independently. Equality in Coaching stimulates good thinking. And thinking is the point.

So in the Contracting conversation you as coach may want to say things like:

My role as coach is to help you to think for yourself.

My role as coach is *not* to do your thinking for you.

The issues and questions you bring to the coaching sessions are best addressed and explored by you, not by my interpretation of you or your situation, nor by my knowledge of human beings or oganizations.

I will offer you my insights and perspectives and other tools only after you have had suffcient time to come up with your own, often better, ideas, thoroughly, and only if you specifically ask me to.

The session is successful if your ideas, directions, insights, questions and feelings are all better than mine.

My expertise is a process of behaving with you in ten ways that will keep you thinking for yourself through a particular quality of Attention and a naturally constructed sequence of questions. Are there any of these Ten Components of a Thinking Environment that concern you?

The key obstacles in your life and work emerge from the key obstacles in your thinking. These obstacles are nearly always untrue limiting assumptions. When appropriate you will find and remove those assumptions.

Equally, it is often in the silence that the best ideas emerge.

I will be operating from a particular view of human nature and inherent life. This view I call the Positive Philosophical Choice. It asserts that you are inherently intelligent, free to make real choices about your life and your feelings, able to think about anything, loving, aware of others, eager for solutions good for everyone, creative and worthy of good outcomes. This philosophical choice will guide my behaviour and my responses during our sessions.

You also, of course, in the contracting session, and on paper later, establish the frequency and cost and location of the sessions. That and other logistical things go without saying.

And just in case you do not already have a refined set of questions to determine the client's goals, (and the payer's goals), for the coaching experience, these might guide you:

What do you want to achieve for yourself or your organization through these coaching sessions?

What changes or developments will you consider to be signs of success of the coaching?

What other coaching experiences have you had? What was valuable about them? What was not?

Do you expect your sessions to have an emotional component occasionally? How comfortable are you with your own feelings?

What background about you, your organization, your job performance and/or the way your colleagues experience you do you think I need to know in order for the sessions to be of most value to you?

Are your personal goals for the sessions different from your organization's or your employer's goals for your sessions?

Are there psychometric tools or other processes you would like to include as part of the coaching?

What would you want these sessions to be sure not to include or to aim for?

How much do you know about the Thinking Environment approach to coaching? Which aspects of it do you particularly want in these sessions? Which aspects do you not want?

And don't take notes. Even in this pre-session session. The contracting session is a session. You are characterizing Attention. You have to *be* it as you describe it. You will remember most of what they say anyway. And you can write down a few notes after they are gone – after they are in the car, turning out of your drive, reflecting on that unexpected, ineffable but invaluable experience of thinking for themselves because you were wholly present.

That's the contracting bit. It is a treasure of a free gift.

CHAPTER 41

How's It Going?

Coach Supervision In A Thinking Environment

Okay, you hate the term. It brings to mind scrutinizing overseers and Saturday school detention. Independent thinking? Forget it.

I don't particularly like the term myself. But let's get over it. It is here to stay. (I did not like the term "coaching" when it first caught on, either. But it has settled down for me now and has developed its independent connotation of human development, not just sports. Anyway, the field of coach supervision is growing like mad. And that is a good thing.)

So let's refresh its definition. Supervision (think: Super-Vision) is the act of seeing the valley. Coach supervision allows the coach to think about their coaching. It is, as Peter Hawkins said, "a time for coach and supervisor regularly to review and monitor the coach/client relationship." It is a place to figure out the hard places – in their practice, in their response to certain clients, in their discomfort with particular topics or areas that the client may need to explore, in the organizational context of their coaching, in their skill and knowledge gaps. It is a coach's time to think. And it is a supervisor's time to appreciate, reflect with, challenge and encourage the coach. And it can be a delight. Especially if you do it in a Thinking Environment.

Shirley Wardell, in her Masters thesis on coach supervision, says compellingly that a Thinking Environment raises the effectiveness of supervision and makes it a pleasure. The supervision takes place, of course, with all Ten Components as the supervision culture. And it can follow roughly the six-part Thinking Session, allowing for Part II to be a time when the supervisor has more input and direction, by invitation from the coach.

Also, the opening question focuses directly on the coach's coaching: "What from your coaching practice would you like to think about today, and what are your thoughts?" The supervisor, maintaining the Thinking Environment, follows up with the "What more?" question so that the coach has maximum opportunity to think for themselves about the issues they have brought to the supervision session.

Finding and replacing untrue limiting assumptions also hugely enhances coach supervision. This is particularly so when the coach needs to explore difficulties with particular clients or with particular topics. The assumption question works fantastically, for example, when the coach has discovered topics they hope their clients won't raise. These topics will hold resonance of pain of some kind for the coach. Getting free of this pain will allow the coach to encourage their clients toward whatever topics they need to explore, rather than subtly deflecting them from certain ones.

"What are you assuming," the supervisor may ask, "that stops you from welcoming this topic?" The sequence of questions can then free the coach to be the best they can be.

Which is the point. Excellence of independent thinking is as much the point of supervision as it is of coaching itself.

Never mind the word. Just remember the valley.

CHAPTER 42

Whose Mind Is It?

Mentoring In A Thinking Environment

"I fired my mentor after two meetings," Denise told me. "She never listened.

"My manager told me I was foolish because that was not the point of mentoring. Anita, my mentor, had experience and power and would open doors for me and show me the ropes and tell me things that would give me an advantage over others. I was supposed to be grateful for that and drink in her every word.

"But I couldn't figure out where *I* was in all of that. It may sound selfish, but I wanted to think about my career and my experience, too, not just hear about hers. And even when she focused on me, it was always with guidance, hardly ever a question. It was boring, actually. Firing her may sideline me in this company, but I don't care. I have better things to do with my lunch hour."

Mentoring is for the mentee. Most of all, for the mind of the mentee. I think that mentoring needs to focus on and develop the mentee's finest independent thinking about their work, their career, their life, their dreams. The mentor's perspective is an important ingredient in this special relationship. But it feeds. It is not the feast.

Noemi Fabry and I spent two years starting from scratch. We met in London regularly to talk about what truly good mentoring could consist of, and to experiment with it. We came up with a design and with a programme to develop it. Several years later, this Time To Think Mentoring Process is working well – probably because it puts the independent thinking of the mentee first.

The Mentoring Session

Here is how it works:

The mentor and mentee meet for two hours per month. Two discrete hours, all theirs, un-distracted. (That rules out lunch.)

They divide the two hours into roughly four stages. During the first stage, the mentee thinks for herself about an issue of her choice. The mentor listens, and continues with their Attention to generate more thinking from the mentee. They remove limiting assumptions if appropriate. They listen, listen, listen, listen. Basically, the mentor gives the mentee a *Thinking Session*. (In practice this usually amounts to a superb Part I only. But over time mentor and mentee can learn the whole Session framework and add more and more precision and quality to their work together.)

During the second stage, the mentee asks the mentor questions. The mentor answers them, succinctly, staying alert to the staying power of the mentee, and not answering questions the mentee did not ask. Simply, the mentee *interviews* the mentor.

During the third stage, the mentee gives the mentor a *Thinking Session*.

During the fourth stage, the mentee and mentor *appreciate* each other. Some do this verbally. Some write it and give it to each other before they leave. Some write it later and mail it to each other. The written appreciations grow into a recorded treasury of affirmation and encouragement. So most people prefer to write their appreciative thoughts right there, before they say goodbye, before the very next day the intention to write wakes up to find itself filed under "sometime", office denial-speak for "never".

Many people report liking this as a kind of template of appreciation:

Our Session today was well worth the time because:

Time is what people risk in investing in mentoring. Both people have to think it is worth their time; and so does the organization. So reflecting on time seems to be a good way to reflect appreciatively on the person.

Equality vs Diversity

Mentoring in a true Thinking Environment is an experience of all Ten Components. But most fascinating to me is the confluence of Equality and Diversity. Aren't they incompatible? Noemi and I wondered about this for ages. Can you hold this particular form of Diversity – the differences in age, experience, status, influence, knowledge, identity group, expertise – in positive tension with Equality? Are people with more or less of something than each other truly equals?

Yes.

If I am your mentee, you may be older and more senior and have greater influence than I do at the moment, and know things I don't know; this is some of our diversity. But I am your equal just the same. I am your equal as a thinker, as a person of value to this company, as a contribution to the planet. And my thinking matters as much as yours.

Yes, but if I am the mentee, and our mentoring relationship is for me to develop, am I not more important than you in this relationship? Conversely, if I am to be learning from your experience and power and knowledge, aren't you more important than I am in this relationship?

No.

We need each other equally for our mentoring to work best. And that is the challenge. We have to begin by regarding each other as equals. We continue by regarding each other as equals. And we end by regarding each other as equals. Only then do we both benefit from the differences, the diversity, the differentials. (Does paradox ever *not* show up in Thinking Environments, I ask you?)

The participants on our first organizational Mentoring Programme taught me this in a particular way. I thought I had figured it out. To keep the mentee the focus on the one hand, but the mentee and mentor equals on the other, the process, I assumed, should have only three stages: A Thinking Session for the mentee and the Interview with the mentor. Then appreciation.

But within the first three months of the programme, all of the mentees around that table were telling me that they felt *unequal* to the mentors because they, the mentees, did not get to be the Thinking Partner for the Mentor. "Really?" I asked them? "Wouldn't that then shift the balance and give more airtime to the mentor?"

"No," they insisted. "It would give more expertise time, make-a-difference time, to the mentee. It would put the mentee into a giving role, and that lifts the mentee up, balancing her with the mentor."

"Yes, but wouldn't the mentor feel unwilling to think about her real issues with someone in the company?"

"Sure, sometimes, but so might the mentee, and we each can make choices about what to think about. That is true always."

I could see the light. We tried it. It was brilliant.

So the mentoring process is now in four stages. It now includes the Mentor's Thinking Session. Diversity and Equality, from each to each, equals both.

The Interview is a different story. You might not think that asking and answering questions could be a complex process. What's to go wrong?

Lots.

Here's the challenge: I am the mentee. You are the mentor. I ask. You answer and answer and answer and answer and answer and answer. I lose the will to live.

And here's another challenge: I ask. You interrupt before I fully figure out my question. You answer the wrong question. I simmer.

And another challenge: I ask. You answer a question you wish I had asked. I fume.

And another: I ask. You advise. I resist. I feel stupid. I don't understand why. I fire you.

Lots.

So, we have inoculated the Interview. In the programme both mentor and mentee learn about the cultural tendency for the Mentor to take over and the mentee to take cover. So the mentors learn to be truly interested in the mentee's formulating of the question they want to ask the mentor. And the mentor learns to answer only *that* question. And, most important of all, to answer it in words and phrases that *do not advise*. The human mind typically naps during advice, however wide open the eyes. Advice says, "Stop doing your own thinking now; mine is better than yours. Be me."

Very soporific stuff.

"You should" and "If I were you, I would" are the worst. So we discourage those phrases. "My experience was" or "I have learned" are best. We encourage those.

And just barely okay is, "If I were in your situation, I would." That is a slippery option because you will never be in the other person's situation because, well, because no two situations are ever the same, for one thing. But also because one inextricable and enormous feature of the other person's situation is *they*. Which you are not, in case you have forgotten.

And it is not just the mentor who has to learn some things about the simple-looking Interview process. The mentee, too, has to practise listening all the way through the mentor's response, being interested in the fact that they are thinking and in where they will go next, not interrupting or arguing. The mentor needs to think well. So the mentee creates a Thinking Environment for them as well.

But even with that much Thinking Environment from the mentee, the mentor monitors the mentee's interest in their answer, and the minute the mentee looks fadey, the mentor wraps it up and turns their Attention back to the mentee.

"What are you thinking now?" is a good transition back. Or, "Is that a useful answer?" And then, "What other question would you like to ask?"

The interview is elucidating and often very, very helpful to the mentee, and it is a pleasure for the mentor. But it is packed with skill.

Beverly Whitehead conducted research into the effectiveness of the Time To Think Mentoring Programme and process. After six months of working with sixteen mentoring pairs, Beverly's organization reported benefits not only for the mentee, but also for the organization. (Her research is mentioned in the Appendix and is available on the Time To Think website.) Dominance disappeared. Equality showed up everywhere.

But what about all that door-opening and lunch? Do them, too. But not *instead* of the mentoring session. And imbue them both with a Thinking Environment.

In real mentoring, as Beverly's research confirms, the mind of the mentee matters most.

CHAPTER 43

Whose Turn Is It?

Dialogue In A Thinking Environment

Believe it or not, Dialogue in a Thinking Environment can be harder to master than Thinking Pairs. This is the phenomenon of new vs familiar. The dog metaphor aside, it is easier to learn something brand new than to change something familiar.

In a Thinking Pair everything is new because it is not an exchange. It is two people having discrete turns to think about different topics. This is truly unfamiliar. Weird at first, even. But we are willing to learn it, and we learn it easily, and we value it, and we can sustain it because it is not tampering with anything we already know.

But dialogue we know. We do it all of the time. Conversations, chats, exchanges of any kind, back and forth, back and forth: That is familiar. It gets sloppy pretty fast, and most of the time we don't really like the slop, but we tolerate it because that is all there is on offer, and because, well, it's familiar.

And so with Dialogue in a Thinking Environment, we have to tamper. We have to un-learn. And that requires us to, as Willliam Starbuck put it, "engender doubt." We don't like doubt. We prefer certainty. And when it comes to processes that we don't even think of as processes – they are just life, aren't they? – we can get pretty doubtful about doubt.

But dialogue, the way it is usually practised, could do with some doubt.

So when we get brave and decide that, on second thought, we would like to clean things up, we would like to experience the back and forth of dialogue and conversation differently, we would like to think all the way through an idea, for example, and not be cut off at the pass, we require of the dialogue process some changes. And the changes keep butting up against the familiar, and so it is challenging.

But it is worth it. Dialogue in a Thinking Environment is just about the best exchange with a person you can imagine. It disallows interruption; That is the main change. That is big. It asks for genuine interest, even fascination, from the listener. That is also big. It asks for stillness. And Ease. They are huge. And it requires all of this while the listener is also aware that very soon they will be replying, having their own turn, thinking in response to, and building on or challenging, what the other person has just said.

Gorgeous, but very different from Thinking Pairs.

Or maybe not so different, actually. You could say that the listener in a Thinking Environment Dialogue is providing the culture of the Thinking Pair. I think this analogy is useful because it raises the bar of behaviour of the listener during the other person's turn. Thinking Pair listening is up there with Mike Phelps swims and Lang Lang concerts.

So maybe it makes it easer to think of dialogue in a Thinking Environment as being Thinking Pairs back and forth (except, of course, for the mutual topic).

Also, Dialogue in a Thinking Environment is not stiff. It is as lively as sloppy dialogue any day. It just happens also to be more intelligent and more elegant. And it does not burn up its own insides through the adrenalin of interruption. Interruption is an *un*appreciative act causing the flip side of those two appreciation-brain-related things to go into gear: Blood flows less well to the brain; the heart de-stabilizes and thus the cortex is less stimulated; thinking defaults into the boring old task of survival.

Dialogue in a Thinking Environment prevents this receding of fuel to the brain. It is full of Appreciation. Dialogue then becomes alive and robust and fun and profound. Genuine interest from the listener, and the kept promise of no interruption, make this possible.

There is one important act of discipline at the heart of this kind of dialogue, though. Our turn is not just an act of receiving the generous gift of generative Attention. We also take responsibility to remember that this is *not* a Thinking Pair. We do not get the entire allotted time to think and speak. We get only a bit of it.

After a very few minutes we hand over to the other person. We give them generative Attention. Then they hand over to us. And we get a bit more time. This is back *and forth*, remember. And determining when the back turns to forth is a disciplined and thoughtful job. It is the job of the thinker, not the listener. This is the opposite of familiar dialogue where the listener stops listening and charges into the person's turn to snatch one of their own.

So when it is your turn to speak, you stay aware of Equality and make sure to stop so that the other person can have their turn. Their seamless Attention is trusting you to do this. One good way to "hand over" is to ask the question, "What do you think?" And then begin to listen.

(And note: "What do you think?" is a different question from "What do you think about what I have just said?" Think about it. Infantilization, as I said, is sneaky.)

And so, we trust each other: To listen without interruption (and without even a sign of imminent pounce), and to stop and turn over the turn.

This makes possible clean, shimmering dialogue, full of meaning and rich in result.

You both deserve this.

CHAPTER 44

Who Is Listening?

Mediation In A Thinking Environment

There are two people I know who make peace everyday. They help separating and divorcing couples talk to each other. Out of the talk, understanding emerges. And out of the understanding, lives heal.

Actually, it is out of the *listening* that lives heal. John Spiegel and Donna Duquette are professional divorce mediators. As mediators their job is to facilitate communication and promote problem-solving between people in conflict, from the neutral perspective of even-handedness. Breakthroughs in mediation occur, they say, proportionate to the degree of Thinking Environment the mediator sustains. Progress happens when clients are thinking for themselves well.

Thinking is not the first word that comes to mind when you consider conflict. Thinking usually, in fact, makes a quick exit when battles begin. Anger stays in the room. Resentment stays. Old pain and mistrust take the big chairs. But thinking is long gone. And it is thinking that is needed most. But mediators don't always know how to produce it. In that way Donna and John are pioneers in this field.

I am interested in the field of mediation because in the end it is mediation that will establish peace. It will not be the demonizing. Not ultimata. Not bombs. Not security forces. It will be – it always has been – mediation that prevents and heals war, personal or global.

But the reason I include mediation in this book is that all of us are mediators. We don't get paid for it. We don't call ourselves that. And we may not even realize that that is what we are. But it is.

Are you a manager? You are a mediator. Do you have friends? You are a mediator. Are you a parent? You are definitely a mediator. Are you in an intimate relationship? You should be a mediator, even though the job of promoting everyone's clear thinking, when you are one of the parties involved is one of life's greatest challenges. When you can do it, though, the quality of resolution is clean and grown up and good. It produces some of life's sweetest moments.

So we all have a lot to learn from John and Donna.

Mediation's DNA is self-determination. Self-determination means that the participants, not the judges, lawyers or mediators, make the decisions. John and Donna think that the Component of Equality nurtures self-determination. They explain that with Equality in place, both parties know they will have equal time and turns to speak. This very structure then says that each *can* think. The structure says that neither party is more intelligent than the other. In that way, the structure establishes neutrality. Thinking improves. And self-determination has a better chance. They say:

> We can set a tone of Equality by giving equal Attention
> to participants, looking at both during the discussions,
> reflecting the comments of both. If we let one person talk for
> too long, we risk losing the Attention and trust of the other.

Most important, Donna and John have found that, by applying the principles of a Thinking Environment, they can listen with skill and intention that take their mediator-listening to a new level. They also help their clients to listen to each other this way. They don't talk about ground rules. They talk about the importance of good thinking and the impact of listening on thinking. They ask the clients help to make the best thinking happen. This establishes further respect for the clients.

But mediation is a time of pressure and pain, and listening this generously to blaming and judgment can be excruciating. Again, the structure helps. It is sturdy when the human heart wobbles.

John and Donna also encourage the expression of feelings. Expressing feelings lets us think again. Repressing represses just about everything, including thinking. In their words:

> Clients need to know that the mediator has understood the nature of their feelings before they will fully trust the mediation process. Also, they think better if they don't have to pretend they are not struggling. We also share with them the emotional stages of divorce. We explain that emotions do finally change, and mediation can ultimately be successful.

> Participants feel tension and time pressure and pain. And so from the mediator they need Ease, Equality and the Positive Philosophical Choice toward the brilliance of each other's minds and hearts. They need to remember that they are the ones who hold the answers to their challenges.

> They need the mediator not to rush to solutions or press them to move faster. When the mediator gives the gift of their own Ease in the face of their urgency, slowing down makes the process move faster.

Donna's experience says a lot about this:

> During a divorce mediation, I noticed that the wife was quieter than usual. My questions weren't drawing her out. So I decided to caucus with each of them separately. I met with her first.

> "You seem quiet today," I said, "what are you thinking and feeling?" She talked for 15 minutes. She said she was confused. She said she had reservations about the tentative agreements. She said she was afraid of what the future held.

I listened to her. I did not offer advice or express my own perspective. At the end of that time, she was clearer about what she wanted. She knew what was bothering her about the previous decision. She was now ready for discussion.

I asked the husband to come in. I wanted to give equal time in private caucus. He stood directly in front of my chair. With his hands clenched, he told me he was in a rage. He assumed his wife's silence meant she no longer wanted to negotiate. For ten minutes he expressed anger and fear and pain. I said nothing, and instead relaxed into my chair. I kept eye contact and communicated my full Attention. Then he sat down.

I asked him what he wanted. I asked him to consider other possibilities for his wife's silence. I then met with them both. Within a half-hour, they had reached agreement on the remaining issues.

I am convinced that those agreements would not have happened without the chance for them, with my full listening Attention and Ease, to think out loud and express their strong feelings without interruption.

The combination of Equality and *Attention* is needed especially during the most heated dialogue between parties. The Timed Talk process (see *Time To Think*, page 120) of the Thinking Environment can be perfect to help two (or more) people, furious at each other, say what they think and feel and move toward good ideas and an ease of tension:

When participants are having difficulty listening or giving each other space to talk, we can try Timed Talk, where they will each have a three-minute turn to speak, going back and forth for many turns. Each knows they will get their turn at the end of the other's three minutes. It starts out rugged and raw. But it becomes civil and sometimes very creative.

Does it surprise you that woven through all of this is Appreciation? Appreciation helps everything. But you can imagine that in conflict it seems almost counterintuitive. How do you as a mediator keep focused on the good things in the participants when at least one of them is being very diffcult? And how do you help them appreciate each other when at the moment they nearly hate each other? By staying intelligent yourself.

In front of you are real, complex, resourceful, kind people. They are hurting. But their hurt is not their essence. So you make the decision to trust their intelligence and their inherent desire for mutually good solutions. That is a challenge. But it is your job. And nothing else works anyway.

> Early on we face the clients toward the positive things in their lives, and even in their relationship. From the first meeting we ask parents what puts a smile on their faces regarding their children. We ask them to tell us something positive about their children that has happened recently. And even what they appreciate about the other's parenting. We watch them relax a bit. We see the trust rise a bit. And we notice their thinking improving.

> We also catch any positive statements that one participant makes about the other. We stop the conversation and repeat those appreciative words to ensure that the participants heard them.

> At the end we appreciate the participants for their patience, diligence, organization and honesty. They then think better between meetings and come again having progressed to a better place.

Appreciation is the workhorse of mediation.

Questions are, too. John said it this way:

> I teach mediation. I have always encouraged mediators to ask
> questions rather than make statements. Making statements
> risks undercutting neutrality (as perceived by clients) and
> also pulls the focus away from the client's good thinking.
> From my understanding of the Thinking Environment, I now
> make an even more useful statement: "In general the human
> mind works best in the presence of questions."

And, as always, especially in conflict, assumptions, untrue and limiting, swarm and sting and gnaw on the strategies and ideas being built in the sessions. Questions, especially Incisive Questions, protect and rescue these ideas.

These questions have worked well:

> If you were over being angry about the affair, what do
> you think you would say about the parenting plan?

> What do you want to achieve at this point?

> What are you assuming that is limiting your ability to
> resolve this issue?

> What do you really think?

> If you put yourself at the centre of the universe, what
> would you want?

> If you could suddenly feel confident about processing
> numbers, what would you think about this proposal?

For example, during one mediation session the couple could not figure out an appropriate alimony amount. The discussion went in circles until we asked, "What are you assuming that is stopping you from reaching agreement on the alimony issue?"

Without any hesitation, the wife blurted out, "It isn't the money. How else will I know if he cares or ever cared about me?" I think the answer surprised even her. The discussion that followed was much more productive.

Place matters, too. People can't think well in conflict if the place they are meeting says: "You don't matter here; only the mediator matters; only the lawyers matter; only one of you matters."

> As soon as our clients walk in the door, they know that
> they matter. Our office welcomes them. It soothes them.
> They sit in comfortable chairs around a low round table.
> They see a setting for a conversation, not for combat.

Donna and John also recognize that clients from the first minute do best if they understand the structure of the mediation relationship, including the structure of a Thinking Environment:

> Mediators always begin their relationship with clients by
> talking about mediation as a structure, a structure different
> from the structure they have been using to communicate
> with each other up to now. But we go a step further now.
> We also make visible the Thinking Environment structure.

> We start by talking explicitly about the bigger picture of
> wanting the best thinking from everyone in the room. We
> talk about how certain kinds of behaviour promote good
> thinking. We communicate the principles of the Thinking
> Environment and specific behaviours that we know will
> help good thinking, and specific behaviours that hinder. We
> like to describe the Ten Components as the compass. And
> the various ways to apply the Components as the map.

John and Donna say also that mediators need time in the office each day to think for themselves about any issue of their choice, to be listened to without interruption. They have made short daily Thinking Sessions standard in their practice. In addition, when a crisis arises in a mediation (or in some aspect of their mediation practice), they make time for this generative listening, so that they can bring their best thinking to solving the crisis.

If John and Donna's success is any indication, it would seem that mediation cries out for the finest thinking between parties, and that, therefore, the mediator's first responsibility to them is to create a Thinking Environment.

Roads to peace will always take discipline. The key discipline will be the one that keeps people thinking beautifully. That discipline will eventually lift them into wanting the best for all parties. They will soon stop wanting to win. They will start wanting an intelligent, loving world.

CHAPTER 45

How Do We Get Out Of This?

Couples And Interlocking Assumptions

It was 4am. We were awake. Not wide. But awake. I decided to capitalize on the moment. "Darling, could you help me think about this workshop I am doing for couples?" I asked Christopher. He murmured something I interpreted as, "Certainly."

So I reached for my notebook. "Here is what I have so far." I read him my outline. "What do you think could improve it?"

"Well," he said audibly, "it is very powerful. But you don't have anything in it about interlocking assumptions."

I sat straight up. "What are those?"

"You know," he said, "the assumptions that entwine and cause the chronically stuck places in a relationship. In those places neither person can move, and so that stuckness recurs again and again. The stuckness is actually just two untrue assumptions wound around each other."

"How do you know all of this? I have never heard of this before."

"Sure you have," he said gently. "We figured it out the weekend we met. The last day, remember? In the library."

I thought back. That had been a magical weekend. And I knew he was referring to the afternoon when, after falling in love and being together every chance we could in and out of a conference I was leading, we had a last time alone among the books. I remembered the amazing question we asked each other, wanting to create a path for this relationship to be the best of our lives.

What do we each know about ourselves that could cause
diffcult moments in our relationship?

Christopher said, "I get distant when a person gets emotionally needy."
I said, "I get emotionally needy when a person gets distant."

Tell me, how interlocking is that?

I saw at that crazy hour what Christopher had seen 22 years earlier:
2 assumptions, entwined, as tight as Passion Flowers. But not as pretty.

We to this day are grateful for the understanding of these two emotional
patterns. And I finally understood that they arise from two assumptions.
Dawn came in a hurry that day.

Assumptions like those (and it turns out that millions, well lots, of
people have those two assumptions to deal with in their relationship),
kicked off at the same time, create a recurring, painful impasse. For
happiness to resume, the assumptions have to unlock. Fortunately,
Incisive Questions can help with that.

So, I learned afresh that morning that in any relationship people bring
to each other not only their strengths and healthy perspectives, but also
their various dysfunctions. We bring, in other words, both our true
liberating assumptions about human nature and how life works; and
our untrue limiting assumptions.

Our success in a relationship stems from the interlocking true liberating
assumptions. Our disappointments and unresolved conflict in the
relationships stem from the interlocking untrue limiting assumptions.

Understanding each other entails understanding these assumptions. And
we need, in order to increase happiness and success in the relationship,
to help each other identify those assumptions and replace them with true
liberating ones that can free us to relax and love each other all the more.

For example, generating the interlocking patterns of emotional
distance/emotional neediness are often the assumptions: 1) I cannot
stay connected to myself when another person is emotionally too needy;
and 2) I am nothing without that person. These assumptions are not

inherently true. Their liberating alternatives would be something like: 1) My connection to myself is inviolable; and 2) I am whole always.

Assumption Question   Incisive Question

What are you assuming that is causing this stuck place between you?

I cannot stay connected to myself when a person is emotionally too needy.

I am nothing without this person.

If you knew that your connection to yourself is inviolable, *how* would you get unstuck?

If you knew that you are whole always, *how* would you get unstuck?

Interlocking Limiting Assumptions   Interlocking Liberating Assumptions

While we are on the subject of couples, one crucial thing: listen.

Another crucial thing: listen.

Give up interrupting each other forever. Today.

And make sure you have roughly (but not too roughly) equal turns to speak.

Unlocking interlocking assumptions is all well and good. Fabulous, actually. But if you cannot listen to each other, warmly with discipline, eagerly with interest, even when you are locked tighter than those Passion Flowers, progress is slow. And the tendrils lift their heads, greedy.

You gain everything by staying interested in what your partner really thinks and feels. You gain nothing by cutting them off, or becoming a talk marathon yourself.

Intelligent coupledom is the richest thing humans ever thought up. But it takes exactly that, intelligence, to make it work well. And untrue limiting assumptions are stupid. So don't believe them. Don't count on them to guide you. And don't act on them. Find the true liberating ones to replace them, and use them to *think* instead.

Love is a fine act of thinking.

And intelligent feelings are the sweetest feelings of all.

Part Two

In Practice

In Groups

CHAPTER 46

How Many Does It Take?

Introducing Group Applications

"Groups," I said, in an interview.

Charles had asked me, "What has been for you the most surprising development in the unfolding of the Thinking Environment?"

I thought of stories of personal transformation. I thought of goals and dreams realized. I thought of interviews and advisors and doctors and national Presidents and even golf champions. I thought of insight and innovation and individual reassertion of choice. I thought of love.

But actually, the thing that for me has been most surprising is the embracing of the Thinking Environment by groups. From years of working with people in pairs and seeing the disrobing of victimization, however sleek the suit, then to see that same liberation in groups has been a surprise to me. I don't think everyone has been surprised by this. Maybe I am just a bit cynical about groups and their chimeric tendencies. Groups can be creepy. They can disappear people. Groups can become inured to things that individuals cannot stomach. Groups are not famous for their fine thinking.

But in the end groups are in fact individuals, linking. And I guess that when the individual is more important than the link, the link becomes another catalyst for intelligence and humanness. Anyway, it seems so.

Because when groups structure themselves as Thinking Environments, when the individual intelligence shines, very good things happen. I have seen this time and time again.

I am less cynical now.

CHAPTER 47

How Would It Be?

Thinking Environments At Work

In fact, I have had some unforgettable moments. As the Thinking Environment has taken hold in more and more groups and organizations, I have seen extraordinary things. Most moving for me has been, in the faces of leaders, a kind of irrepressible quickening, an acknowledgement of something in front of them that was remarkable.

Before their eyes people became even brighter, more articulate and acquainted, sometimes for the first discernible time, with a measure of humility. In front of them also the quietest, assumed to have nothing to contribute, sharpened, spoke, engaged, became invaluable.

In front of these leaders ideas were born that they knew would before have been out of reach. These ideas had found the right environment in which to advance beyond a single cell – no longer aborted by the dynamics of the group.

I have also seen in the faces of teams a relaxing of the muscles of defence. I have seen diversity – of ideas and identities – no longer ambushed by take-no-prisoners ambition in others. Into their midst I have watched arrive a no longer occasional visitor: Dignity. And in the eyes of these teams I have seen, as in their leaders, excitement woven with relief.

I have watched conversations of every kind grow smarter, sharper, more rigorous, more generous – both more stimulating and more at ease, rich in original thinking, grounded in good information and more open-armed.

I have seen groups set free to find the best ideas in the most unusual places, where the gems in the independent thinking of people finally catch the light.

It has been good.

How might you make this happen? With your influence, what can you do to make this much difference?

Let's start with early morning. Before getting out of bed, picture each person you are likely to be with today. Remember that each of them has a wondrous mind, unique, eager to be ignited. Be curious about what those amazing minds might generate if you ask them what they think, and then listen without interruption, interested.

Stay curious about that as you dress. Remember that they are probably dressing, too, and hoping (consciously or not) that today will be the day you want them to think for themselves, with you. Imagine how much they want to think of things they have not thought of before because of the trucks that people, sometimes possibly you, usually drive through their ideas, hour after hour, every day.

Then before you get to work, offer yourself a Thinking Environment, choose an issue you are dealing with. Ask yourself a question: What do I really think about this? Or: What do I really want here? Or maybe: What do I know now that I am going to find out in a year? Or: What am I (or we) assuming that is holding us back? Or: If I knew that there is a way forward that we have not yet thought of, how would I engage everyone on this? Or maybe, having already committed to a way forward, the question would be: Then what? Or maybe, alert to the unsustainability of greed, you might ask: How much is enough?

When someone wants your advice, ask them what they think first. Be so interested in what they will say next that they think of their own brilliant answers. Then if they still want yours, ask them what their question is before you reply.

And throughout the day ask yourself the question: What is the question? Decide to ask.

And to listen. Give *Attention* until the person has finished thinking. Asking questions is good, but not if it is just activity. Not if it is just a way to relieve yourself of the challenge of stillness, and of becoming fascinated. Questions liberate the mind – unless they rush it. Unless they grab it by the neck and drag it in a different direction.

Then when you get to work, notice the people before you notice anything else. Say hello warmly, and then ask a question. It might be just: How are you? But *want* to know. Be interested. This does not have to take long. A few seconds of undistracted engagement accomplishes more than hours of disconnection. And ask another question before you move on. Asking gets people thinking. Our minds shrivel in sandstorms of statement. But as you ask, want palpably to know.

Throughout the day, stop and notice. Take in what is happening. Get the *Information*; and get it from unusual places. Ask the people who are never asked but who know the most. The people on the ground or on the rig, the people with the customer, the people who clear the tables, the people who load the trucks, the people who measure the pulse, the people who grade the papers, who register the guests, who answer the phone, who do the experiments, the people who organize everyone else. And settle in as they speak, because you are interested, because they are thinking.

Ask yourself: What can I do in this moment to *Encourage* people to think for themselves? How do I give them the courage to go to the unexplored edge of their ideas? How do I stop competing with them? Whether or not I agree with them, how do I celebrate them as thinkers?

Then *Appreciate*. Notice what is good and say it. Right then. Notice. Then tell them. Notice what is going well with a group. Tell them all. Notice what is working well around the place. Tell the person who made it happen. Notice what quality you value in the person you are about to see. Tell them.

Notice what is good, and say. Everyone in your path will think better around you all day long if you do.

Let people cry or say they are scared or angry. Give them Attention while they do. They are just *feeling* things. They are not dying. And neither are you.

And tell them in a hundred ways that you like the ways they are *Diverse* from you and each other. Stop worshipping sameness and sycophancy and surrender.

And, most important of all (the other points are also most-important-of-all), give everyone a turn. Recognize their *Equality* as thinkers. Aboriginal people discovered this long before white Europe thirsted for all that land. Let's finally follow their lead. Give everyone a turn.

Raising the quality of thinking in groups is not a technique. It also is not a ritual. It is certainly not liturgy. It is a way of being. And so it is an everyday thing.

And if you were on the receiving end of this culture? Regardless of your status, if you worked in a Thinking Environment organization, what would life be like for you?

It would be good. You would know as you walked in the door that people would be interested in what you really think, on issues big and small.

You would know that people would listen to you without interruption, and that you would do the same – and learn unexpected, valuable things.

You would know that someone, many people even, would notice what is good about you and tell you; that genuine appreciation would, in fact, be commonplace, and problems would resolve well as a result.

You would know that in every meeting people would want to know what you think. You would relax because there would be Rounds so that even the quiet people could think and speak on each item. You would leave the meetings with energy. And with time because they would not last so long.

You would know that you and the organization would not be crushed in the jaws of denial because no one would cover up things to protect the leaders.

You would know that if you made mistakes, people would help you correct them, and they would not marginalize you. You would understand the place of creative mistakes in the journey toward success, and even in the very evolution of life.

And so, you would be at ease inside. You would be unafraid.

And no longer afraid, you would dare to think for yourself again. You would dare to stand up. You would find your voice. You would develop your talent.

You would look forward to the day.

A Thinking Environment organization would be something like that. Something that alive.

I mentioned meetings. Maybe you wish I hadn't. Just the word makes some people, often the most senior, despair. "Death watch" is the phrase I heard one person use to describe it. Death of the mind, he said.

So let's look at what can inject life.

How can meetings become the thing you look forward to most when you go to work?

CHAPTER 48

What Does It Take To Save A Life?

Transforming Meetings

"You have ruined me for other meetings now," said Al, an executive, shaking his head. "I am not sure whether to thank you or blame you."

We laughed. But it isn't funny. Meetings are generally so bad these days that to get through them, we bear up by shutting down. We have stopped feeling because we are stopped from thinking. This tastes bad. And it doesn't much matter how much technology we pour in to disguise the flavour. When people cannot think in meetings, meetings kill – initiative, innovation and insight. And energy.

So when Al said that to me, he was talking about heightened awareness through contrast. Over the years of organizational life he had become numb to the pain of interruption, of rushing his thoughts and fighting to keep his turn, of being trampled by the people who stampeded in order to get noticed, of being dismissed when he ventured difference.

But when all of that disappeared, he felt relief, even joy.

But then, when he had to go to other meetings, forced back into the culture of interruption, domination by a few, stringy Attention, self-promotional exclusion of others and 67 slides waiting for the click, he felt the pain that used to be numbed. Heightened awareness through contrast may be part of being truly alive. But half of it isn't much fun.

Nevertheless, Al decided to thank me – because he decided that as long as he worked at that company, with every shred of leadership and influence he had, he would create Thinking Environments. And before he left, he had succeeded in not having to attend a single meeting that was not that good.

And a few, very simple, things, some of which we have known for a decade but cry out to be underscored and spotlighted, and some of which we have discovered recently, are all it took.

First, he cancelled the meeting – in his mind. Then he required himself to justify re-instating it.

Next, he looked at all of the agenda items and crossed off half of them, all of the ones that could be handled in some other way.

Next he prepared the agenda. He put each agenda item into a question. He did this by figuring out what outcome they needed on that item. He considered these outcomes:

Did they need a decision?

Did they need new ideas?

Did they need to discover the implications of their earlier decisions?

Did they need to say how they felt?

Did they need to hear and consider new information?

Did they need to update each other?

Did they need to face something dangerous?

Did they need to connect?

Whatever the desired outcome, the reason for considering the item in the first place, a question could drive the meeting there. One topic, for example, was: Next Year's Budget. The question was: How can we triple the revenue from our commercial line within 18 months? The phrase "Next Year's Budget" had said precisely nothing. Any mind looking at that phrase would begin to yawn.

The *question*, on the other hand, said precisely everything. Any mind looking at that item would begin to think, even before the meeting began.

Putting each agenda item in the form of a question improved his meetings dramatically. Not hard. Not expensive.

Then he contacted the presenters. He told them they would have only 40 percent of the time allotted for their item. The rest of the time would be for the group to think. He asked them not to use PowerPoint – unless pictures were essential to get across the information. Under no circumstances were they to have slides that just had the same words on them they were saying. And five slides max. And he told them they needed to connect with the group. (See Chapter 52 for more on this disturbing subject.)

The good news, he said, was that they would not be interrupted. He told me later that just that one change, not interrupting the presenter, would have been worth all of the Thinking Environment consulting he had received.

Two days later, he walked into the meeting. He smiled (and always did even on the tough days), thanked people for coming, looking at each person, acknowledging that some people had come from far away and all had come from busy days and heavy demand. And he began by asking people to focus on reality, the good part, the successes. He asked questions like: What do you think is progressing well in our work right now?

He knew the research on Appreciation. He made sure the ratio of positive reality to negative reality was at least 5:1. He wanted to stabilize the heart and stimulate the cortex. And he wanted oxygen to flow to people's brains. So he focused first on the reality of what was good.

Then he told them that the most important thing was for the meeting to generate the best *thinking* from each person in the group, He said that to achieve the best thinking, he would give everyone a turn, systematically in an unbroken Round, to generate their best ideas in answer to the agenda question. He told them that their differences, in their thinking and in their various group identities, were vital to the quality of ideas he wanted from them. Who they were mattered.

And no one would interrupt.

And there would be no discussion until the Round was finished.

And everyone would give the person speaking respectful, interested Attention. They could count on it.

They could pass if they did not want or need to speak, but they would always have their turn. They did those Rounds, and occasionally one was all that was needed.

Next he asked for open discussion when anyone could talk anytime – except when someone else was talking. Open discussion: full, maybe fun, even fierce, always productive because free of interruption.

Then he proposed another Round, asking a question to kick it off, driving now toward the end of that item.

In the middle of all of this, he suggested now and then that they think in pairs, sometimes in dialogue, back and forth, sometimes in discrete turns of three minutes each or so, but always without interruption. And then in a Round he asked them for their freshest thinking, not a re-hash of what they had just said in pairs.

And capturing all of the gems from this? He changed that, too. He asked for a scribe from the group, and proposed that they not write a thing on the flip chart until the person said, "The five words I want you to write are…." The scribe no longer paraphrased, interpreted or wrote while the person was still thinking. So the scribe no longer had power to distort and control the captured ideas. Equality again.

And he asked people to stop treating the flip chart as if it had a brain. He asked them to turn their Attention away from the chart and back to the person thinking. (That was hard as it turned out. People's focus is sucked away by the flip chart. They act as if it is about to say something profound. It isn't.)

Oh, and before all of this, he asked people to turn off (really off) all mobiles and berries and laptops. Attention is powerful. It refuses dilution. It is the one thing the brain cannot multi-task. (Genuflectors to "continuous partial attention", arise and focus.) And it is the key thing in generating good thinking and good outcomes in groups. He wanted it to take its rightful place of power in the group.

He also listened for untrue limiting assumptions in people's comments. "We cannot get the revenue up that much because we have no source of extra capital" was one. "It cannot be done in this time frame" was another.

So he found a true, liberating assumption, information they did not have, and built this Incisive Question: "If you knew that the Directors are likely to consider a short-term injection of capital, how would you triple our revenue in 18 months?"

His meeting structure moved a bit like this: opening success Round; agenda question; short, sharp, engaging presentation; Dialogue; Round; Open Discussion; Thinking Pairs; Round; small groups, Round; Incisive Questions; Round; Open Discussion; summary; decision; action steps.

To conclude the business he asked if there were any burning issues for anyone that would be addressed at another time.

And then he ended the meeting the way he had started: a Round focusing on reality: the good kind. He asked, "What do you think has been a success in our meeting?" He occasionally asked them also, "What quality do you value in the colleague next to you?" People left energized, and thinking.

People talked about Al's meetings. They said there was rarely any boredom, or waste, or viciousness, or discouragement, or reprisal or hopelessness. Instead, they said, there was insight, fun, inclusiveness, creativity, energy, efficiency.

One other remarkable thing: they said Al's meetings were shorter.

Attention was why. And Equality. And Appreciation. And Diversity.

These Components, and the others, make the brain work better. And so, if whatever you are doing is not those things, stop. Stop. Take a breath. And do those ten things.

The research of Emily Havers confirms the experience of leaders like Al. It is impressive in its rigour, and inspiring in its conclusions. A précis of it is in the Appendix, and on the website. Spanning four continents and six sectors, it un-frowns even the most cynical foreheads. They acknowledge the possibilities, and the value of leading this change.

In meetings in which people truly value each other's thinking, and, therefore, truly listen to each other, strategies get formed better; goals get met better; budgets get set better; products and services get delivered better; the quality of work gets to shine.

But more importantly, other things get a real chance, things like respect, inspiration, innovation, engagement, inclusiveness, confidence. Things that go on mattering and delivering.

Even when the Als of the organization are gone.

CHAPTER 49

Where Is The Wisdom?

The Time To Think Council

Scott Farnsworth has done some important things with the Thinking Environment. (You can read about his breakthrough work with advisors in Chapter 57.) But one of the best was dreaming up the Time To Think Council.

We were driving down Universal Boulevard in Orlando. We had just completed a workshop together with 12 professionals, helping them re-define "expert" and refine their Attention for clients. I was letting the southern wind whip through my hair as we drove, memorizing the heat to tide me over in England's "summer". Our work had seemed more than innovative enough to me for one day. I was letting down.

But Scott does not take time off from creativity. This drive turned out to be a milestone for the Thinking Environment.

"I've been thinking," he said, "about how one person might receive the wisdom of a group and still keep thinking independently – how 12 or so people could address one person's question without ever infantilizing that person."

I perked up, and closed the window.

"Here's how it could work, I think: One person is the Facilitator. One person is the Presenter. One person is the Scribe. Or there could be a digital recorder. The Presenter identifies an issue or dilemma. They think about it out loud. After a few minutes, maybe not more than ten, they consider what question they would like the people in the group to answer. They formulate the question clearly.

"The Facilitator then confirms the question. They ask the group if they have questions to clarify the Presenter's question.

"After that quick Round, the Facilitator then confirms the question and then poses it to the group, beginning a Round. Somebody volunteers to be first to answer, staying focused on that question only. They speak from their experience. They offer any information they have. They never say, 'I think you should' or, 'If I were you, I would.' They say, 'I have found in my experience,' or, 'Once the following happened to me,' or, 'If I were facing this situation, I would.' Or they give information if they have it. A cousin of the Mentoring Interview.

"The Presenter listens with interest and appreciation, and does not respond or ask questions.

"Everyone in the group, including the Facilitator and the Scribe, has a turn. Each turn is about equal in length.

"The Scribe records on paper the kernel of what each person says.

"At the end of the Round the Facilitator asks the Presenter what their thoughts are now. The Presenter shares perspectives and ideas as the group listens.

"Then each person in the Council says what quality they admire in the Presenter.

"And it is over."

I was ecstatic.

We tried it. It worked superbly. It is about the simplest thing in the world. But its impact is huge.

We decided to call it "The Time To Think Council". We do it every time we work with groups of 15 or fewer. Teams do it, too. And working groups. And people in charge of knowledge-management. And families.

The discipline creates the freedom, so it is important to honour the structure and not to slide into advice. Notice that the Presenter determines what the group addresses. It is not a free-for-all of analysis or projection.

And an amazing thing – some of the best Councils have addressed a Presenter's issue that was way outside the field of the other Council Members. On one occasion the Presenter was the Chief Executive of a gold mining company. The others there were architects. The Presenter's question was, "How do I find and keep gold-mining artisans?" The others in the group had no mining experience at all. But they drew on their experience of finding answers in unusual places and of taking reasonable risks. It was a creative Council and generated in the mining executive three new, successful ideas.

The human mind when focused on a question and given uninterrupted, appreciative Attention can tackle just about anything. And in the Time To Think Council every mind is a gold mine.

CHAPTER 50

Who Makes It Happen?

Facilitation In A Thinking Environment

Facilitators of groups can change the world. I am not kidding.

Consider this: groups gather to make change, nearly always. So, really, they are there to think. Then to be sure something happens from all that thinking. How good their thinking will be has everything to do with how successful their actions for change will be.

Enter: the Facilitator.

Let's say it is you. The group hires you because you are an outsider. You are neutral. You are not threatening to anyone there. You have a front row seat at the top of the hill, so you don't have to keep flushing the detail from your eyes. But you also have good binoculars to spot the detail that matters. You are there for balance.

You are also expected to keep the dominant people from dominating, and the shy people from shying away. And you are there to capture and organize and do that magical thing of presenting back to the group the cleaned-up conglomeration of people's ideas so that the group can decide what to do, and do it.

That all takes a lot of skill and some courage and usually a fair amount of knowledge of the subject, a certain amount of grace, as well as a sense of humour. And some flair. Facilitation is a fine act of engineering.

Enter: The Thinking Environment. Engineering becomes art. Actions for change become people for change.

As a facilitator creating a Thinking Environment you do not formally teach the group how to run their meetings this way. You run it for them.

But you have a cultural impact, nevertheless. You generate truly superb thinking and in the same moment immerse people in equality, imbue people with self-respect and meaning, smarten up everyone's relationship with each other, instil self-confidence, justify hope, double people's energy and demonstrate skills that most people will want to carry away and make a way of life. Not bad for just one day and a sandwich lunch.

To be this kind of catalyst for change, you need only to add these things to your already stellar collection of facilitator skills:

Tell people that good thinking is the aim, and that everyone's thinking matters and that the structure of the meeting will reflect those principles

Present the agenda items as questions

Do an opening success Round

Do agenda item Rounds (always starting with a question)

Do open discussion without interruption

Get people thinking about assumptions

Ask Incisive Questions

Get people thinking in pairs

Get people thinking in small groups, with Rounds

Get people after small groups to share their freshest thinking, not report on what was said

Capture ideas in people's own words

Have people appreciate each other's good qualities

Eliminate mobiles, berries and laptops

Eliminate PowerPoint or keep it three slides max with 60 percent white space

End with a success Round

Group Facilitation in a Thinking Environment can be simply beautiful. Let me tell you about Judy Oliver and Sara Hart.

I had this glimpse into Judy's work:

A colleague asked me to facilitate a group of medical experts and professors. The question was: What does medical professionalism mean in the 21st century?

The group had taken evidence from people. But they had not gelled as a team. They also felt overwhelmed by all the data. My colleague asked me to help on both counts.

According to my sources the group members were extremely bright and experienced, potentially inflexible, traditional and single-minded. I tried not to think about that. I did wonder, though, how they would take even to an Opening Round.

I arrived at the high-tech venue. I pushed all the tables up against the wall. The 14 chairs, one for each group member, I put in a circle in the middle. One man arrived early. He squeezed himself in behind a table. When I invited him to sit in the circle, he was clearly already out of his comfort zone, and it was only nine o'clock.

The others arrived. I invited them to share their names and their job title, and to answer this question: What is it about being a member of this group that most delights you?

After a distinct drawing in of breath, the first person started.

He looked around at the group and admitted how daunted he had felt about being asked to join as he knew that the other people were so experienced and academically accomplished. He expressed pride in being part of the group and in their goal. He said how pleased he was to contribute to it.

I was relieved. He had set a superb standard of authenticity. Others followed similarly. This group of bright, experienced experts became a group of human beings, able to say what they had felt for months but had had no vehicle for. One by one they shared their thoughts, their fears and hopes. Everyone expressed appreciation about being part of the group. Everyone gave spellbound Attention.

How long does the opening Round take for 14 people? Usually only minutes, but this one took well over an hour. I wondered if we could possibly finish this ambitious agenda. But as I listened, I felt a quiet confidence that this needed to happen.

The purpose of the group was to examine and re-define what it means to be a medical professional. So I asked the group this question: What does the world assume currently about the medical profession that tends to limit its impact? There were a few quizzical looks.

And I proposed Thinking Pairs. This was new to them. Their meetings to date had been traditional – large table, lots of paper and lots of formality.

I explained the structure. They practised Attention, Equality and Ease and then delighted in a further exchange of Appreciation within their pair. They laughed shyly and started to relax.

I then invited them to think in small groups about the question. What comes freshly to mind about these limiting assumptions?

Within minutes their ideas tumbled out. They shared the stereotypes – the assumptions – that would need to change in order for the world's view of the medical profession to change.

I invited them to consider this question: "What do you *want* people to assume about the medical profession?" Again in two small groups they had equal turns to think. They then wrote the liberating, true assumptions on the other side of the page.

I asked them to read out the new, positive list. Their energy resembled a marketing department with a new brand!

I pointed out that they had stated the group's true aim: to produce not a good report only, but rather a good report that would remove the untrue limiting assumptions people have about the medical profession. A report that would offer assumptions that are liberating, meaningful and inherently true.

They were amazed that the fun they had shared in those 15 minutes had produced a profound piece of practical work. Another liberating assumption had emerged: hard work doesn't have to be hard.

I invited the group to build on this by considering this

Incisive Question: If you knew that you are going to be successful with this project, what would you want to have achieved at the end?

They thought again in pairs. And again, out tumbled passion and ambition expressing, in very real practical terms, the end game.

The group went on to answer the question: What are the key questions that our report will need to answer?

The answers became the chapter headings for the report. They created the questions they would use to help their future witnesses and themselves to think about the key issues.

The room buzzed with ideas and the sheer human delight of getting so much done, so energetically, in so little time.

So, although the Opening Round had taken over an hour, it had been an important investment. It had laid an essential foundation for the rest of the day, and for the months that followed.

Early in the day the group's achievements had surpassed expectations. The level of trust between them had grown. They had thought with every person in the group. They had given and received appreciation. They knew each other as human beings.

The final report made people, lots of people round the country, think.

A year later people met to look at the question: How is the doctor/patient relationship changing in the 21st century?

They invited me again, but this time to facilitate from
the beginning!

Judy does this all of the time. I wish we had space here to tell you about the neighbourhood group with young and old that went from scornful to powerful as they designed change that would affect every resident. Or the merger that quickly turned from hostility, wariness and disengagement to trust and collaboration because of the Thinking Environment she created among them.

But space is short, and I want to tell you about Sara. You may have heard of The Anita Borg Institute for Women and Technology. Sara conducted over 30 Innovation Workshops for them that included more than 800 participants. She assembled women of all ages: Executives, cleaners, teachers, students, cashiers, radio broadcasters, professors, traffic wardens.

They met to answer the question: What technology would you invent that the community would find helpful? She facilitated these groups always in a Thinking Environment. She told me about this:

Astonishingly, these groups generated over 1,500 ideas.
More than 120 student projects flowed from these
ideas. I'm convinced that the amazing productivity of
these workshops came from our using Thinking
Environment processes.

Each workshop lasted six to eight hours. In the first hour
I taught the Thinking Environment. Because of time,
I taught only four of the ten Components: Attention,
Appreciation, Equality and Ease. We had two Rounds of
thinking in pairs and closed this teaching segment with an
exchange of Appreciation.

I devoted the remainder of the workshop to brainstorming

new ideas. I reminded people frequently to sustain a Thinking Environment. We conducted all small and large group work that way.

As you might imagine, I have fond memories of these workshops. I remember the time when an 11-year-old girl and a 70-year-old retired professor ended up as Thinking Partners. At the end of the workshop, each remarked on how amazing it was to have regarded one another as equals during their time together.

I also remember the workshop in which the "community" was three local schools, and our "community participants" were one hundred 9–14-year-olds. To watch a 12-year-old boy try and *succeed* – after much giggling and blushing – at being a good Thinking Partner was very special.

My fondest memory remains the day we worked with an agency that helped disabled people learn new job skills. In the first moments I realized that many participants could not see; many others could not hear; and several spoke very little English. I pondered the essential component of Attention and wondered how all of this would work.

I had completed my introductory remarks. I explained the processes of a Thinking Environment, why it is important, and how Attention, Equality, Ease and Appreciation generate good thinking. I then gave instructions for the first Thinking Pairs.

And then, suddenly, something like the following came out of my mouth: "For those of you who can't see, we will flash the lights when it's time to switch Thinker and Thinking Partner roles. And for those of you who can't hear, we'll clap our hands." There was a pause, and then the room erupted in laughter. From then on, the day was a joy.

People generated brilliant ideas. And during the final Round people expressed immense gratitude for how valued they had felt during the day. I was then certain of the power of a Thinking Environment. And I reflected on the fact that the impact is strong even if you can't see, or hear or speak fluently the language of your Thinking Partner. Apparently, Attention, Appreciation, Equality and Ease can be *felt*, and are, therefore, generative, if they are genuine.

Sara facilitates many groups and always this way. She does it because it creates an innovative culture in the group. And because of the joy.

You can see these pictures of facilitation. People are thinking. People are appreciative. People are energetic. People are equal. People are building trust. People begin to consider sharper, newer, better ideas and work on them together. Things are changing.

Maybe even the world.

CHAPTER 51

When Does It Hurt?

Resistance And Addiction

Become a Thinking Environment for people, and almost everything gets better. So who would ever decide not to do it?

It's funny, but some people do. Now and then someone, experiencing the process, says, "No." And sometimes it is not, "No, thank you."

I saw this close up once at a corporate Christmas concert. I walked into the room where several members of the team I had taught that year were gathered for pre-performance drinks. It had been three months since we had seen each other. The first eight people were friendly. We shook hands and began to talk. But when Howard arrived, he said to me, "Oh, yes, Nancy Kline. How nice to see you in conditions under which I am not being tortured." (Where is your mother when you need her?)

This reaction fascinated me. Torture? Discomfort, okay; but torture? If the process works so well, what is it about it that could generate that remark?

I am entertaining a theory about this. I am beginning to think that this "torture" is withdrawal from three addictions simultaneously. Addiction to:

Control
Urgency
Certainty

This triumvirate seems to drive the feelings and behaviour of some people so vigorously they cannot bear to be without it. They define their leadership almost entirely in its terms. And as with any addict, to be forbidden the "substance" is to set up your life to search madly for it.

Control, urgency and certainty. All three, addictive. All three, destructive. The behaviours that keep these states in place are exactly the behaviours that stifle independent, rigorous, creative thinking. They do not work. But they can become exactly the way some people conduct relationships and groups over and over again.

The Thinking Environment replaces control, urgency and certainty with:

Respect
Ease
Interest

When you are in a Thinking Environment, you get to figure out what you really do think, and to say it. You get to ask the unspoken questions. You get to contribute to often brilliant answers. You get to notice that your thinking really does matter.

And the reason you can do all of this in a group that might before have been a bear pit, complete with dominance by a few, silence among others, and depleting, disappointing discussion all around, is that everyone is treating you with respect, ease and interest; not with control, urgency or certainty.

But Howard, conceivably a control/urgency/certainty addict, becomes more and more desperate when required to provide you with respect, ease and interest. As you speak, he is waiting, not listening. He wants one thing: his turn. He is assuming that his ideas and experience and analysis are better than anything you could come up with during the uninterrupted Attention he *has* to give you. He assumes he would save time by rushing you. He assumes that hacking up an idea before it is formed will somehow improve it. He sits in the sweat of his own adrenalin, forbidden by the Thinking Environment structure to express it by charging head down, horns protruding, into your sentence.

He assumes that if he listens too long, he will hear things he does not know how to handle, and that he will look stupid in the face of his uncertainty. He assumes that if everyone can think for themselves, he will lose control over the outcome, and that that is bad. He assumes that there is only so much success to go around, and that if you shine, he cannot.

Addictive behaviour of any kind is held in place with denial. And this tripod of control, urgency and certainty is no exception. Denial, as we have seen in Chapter 8 is the assumption that what is not happening is happening and that what is happening is not happening. People craving control, urgency and certainty cannot see what is right in front of them. They mistake Rounds and uninterrupted discussion for lack of spontaneity. They confuse listening with doing nothing. They are bored where others are engaged and fascinated. They are in withdrawal. The Thinking Environment is torture.

Most of today's advanced leadership skills rely on the Ten Components of a Thinking Environment to be achieved. They work. They produce both business results and human flourishing. They are the epitome of sanity. So the leader who finds them torture may want to turn from their ramparts and look soberly at the detritus washing up on their shores.

In fact, Howard, if you knew that your best business allies are Respect, Ease and Interest, how would you run your next meeting? How would you feel while your Attention generates others' good thinking? What impressive business outcomes might result?

And, even, what might change in your life?

CHAPTER 52

Are We Connected?

Speaking With Authenticity

"Public speaking was the number one phobia listed on a poll recently. Death was second. Which raises the question: For whom should you feel most sorry at a funeral – the dead person, or the person doing the eulogy?"

So begin Michael Charlesworth and Serena Evans on the subject of a process they call, "Speaking With Authenticity". They have figured out the secret to brilliant public speaking: to do it well you have to be a Thinking Partner for the audience.

This is what they say:

> Treat the entire audience as the Thinker. Give them the finest Attention. Keep your eyes on their eyes.
>
> See yourself and them as Equals. Demonstrate this by speaking loud enough. (This is an area of often huge self-development. Being loud enough requires us to know that we matter and that it is all right to take up space and draw Attention to ourselves, no matter what our parents said.)
>
> Breathe. This is not as easy as you think.
>
> Appreciate the audience, literally in words at the beginning, and with your Attention and your face throughout. Why? Because people, including audiences, get more blood to the brain when they are appreciated. That matters if you want people to think well as you speak.

Don't compete with them; champion their excellence, and your own.

Speak the truth. Speak from your heart, as you, in your real voice, slowly, feeling whatever you feel, happy for the audience to, too.

Tell stories.

Use verbs.

So, in a word? Connect.

Connect. Connect. Connect.

And, as they said, breathe. And as I said, this is not easy. What passes for breathing in our world is actually little more than a drive-by relationship with air. But Serena can ease you into its complexities. (Did you know you can get a Master's Degree in breathing?)

Let's go back for a moment to their instruction to get loud. It turns out that this is not a simple suggestion like, get dressed or get dinner. It, too, is complex, more like, get over it. What lies beneath the quiet voice speaks reams. It may not by now surprise you that the "beneath" is filled with untrue limiting assumptions.

Sometimes Michael and Serena help people find those assumptions so that the person can someday be loud when truly they right now cannot. Not *will not*. Truly *cannot*. The amount of force necessary to get the amount of air necessary through the larynx to produce loud just can't be summoned by the person. Not while they are at the assumption's knife point. But Incisive Questions change all of that.

Jemez stood in front. He spoke for three minutes. No one more than five feet away could hear him. He tried again. He thought he was much louder. He wasn't. He tried again. He breathed in more. He blurted out a 20 percent louder sound and then scuttled back into the same soft volume. He could not believe it when they said it was not louder. Serena asked him this question, "What are you assuming that is making it hard to be loud?"

Jemez thought in silence a long time. Then he said, clearly repressing tears, "I am remembering when I was five. I was at the top of the stairs. I was supposed to be in bed. But I was hurting in my stomach. I came out of my room calling for my parents who were downstairs. Frightened to go down, I just sat there calling and crying.

"Finally, my mother came to the bottom of the stairs. She looked up and said to me, nicely enough I think, but devastatingly, 'Until you stop being so loud, and promise never to be loud again, I will ignore you.'

"I learned in that moment that speaking softly is what it takes not to be abandoned."

Jemez had found the untrue limiting assumption that had closed his voice, potentially forever. But on this day he began to open it. Serena asked, "If you knew that your wholly audible presence is completely good, how would you deliver your three-minute speech?" He knew immediately.

And he resolved to try it alone in the car for a few weeks. And in the shower. Step by step, steps of his choice, he reclaimed the fullness of his voice, of his message, of his relationship with his audience.

Incisive Questions are our key to so many doors, including the one that leads out onto the stage.

And a moment on a very different, but equally debilitating feature of our "speaking" lives I turn (again) to ubiquitous PowerPoint.

As Al discovered in his meetings, the questions are: Can you use it and still stay connected to your audience? How do you keep an audience thinking well in the presence of the screen and all those slides?

Beats me. Beats a lot of researchers, too. PowerPoint has not been demonstrated universally to increase learning. And almost no one stays connected to their audience once the screen comes down, and the slides go up.

We sometimes do need graphs and illustrations in order to grasp a concept. But those can be on paper. And when people are looking at paper, you are still connected to them. They look up; you are there. They look down; you are still there. But they look up at the screen, and they slide right past you. Connection in most PowerPoint presentations is jerky at best. Junk at worst.

What we never need, in fact nearly truly die of, is slides saturated with bullet points and the same words we are speaking. Z-z-z-z-z-z-z-z-z-z-z-z-z-z.

So move slowly toward the injunction to use PowerPoint. Require the people you lead to get good without it. And save some brains along the way.

But if you can use PowerPoint as seamlessly and with as much audience connection as Al Gore did in *An Inconvenient Truth*, go for it.

Otherwise, get real. If you are going to be a Thinking Environment for your audience, unplug the computer and kick the cables back under the table. And when your host asks you ahead of your next presentation what technical support you need in the room, ask for flowers.

Be connected. Be a Thinking Environment. Right there in front of 20 people or 20,000. They are all human beings wanting to do the thing humans do best: Think and feel and learn and determine to do things differently as a result.

But it takes authenticity to get them there. Yours. From the very first minute.

Who's Got The Time?

An Issue Of Behaviour

But doesn't the Thinking Environment just take too long?

No. Surprisingly.

If there is anything counterintuitive about a Thinking Environment, it is that.

Giving everyone a turn in a Round with the mutual promises of no interruption and succinctness, asking, "What more?" in conversations and sessions, quelling urgency inside, saying what is good, focusing on the human mind in front of you – all of this takes less time than rushing, interrupting, dominating and looking away. In fact, time effectively proliferates when you embody the Ten Components.

You could say it this way:

> In a Thinking Environment we think so well in the time
> we have that the time we have increases.

Literally? Not in the there-cannot-be-more-than-60-minutes-in-an-hour kind of way. But effectively, yes. Meetings are shorter. Time (often mountains of it) for correcting mistakes and healing hearts and resurrecting wasted minds is no longer necessary, and so it becomes available for other things. Time for the good things increases.

But I cannot convince you of this through the ink on paper. You will have to try it. And if you do it properly and well, you will grasp the paradox: To take time to think is to gain time to live. These can't-be-true things in life, the things where the figures don't add up but the experience can't be denied, are best left to the Richard Feynmans of the world to explain.

But try it. You might not find that you save 62% of your senior managers' time or do a month of work in 30 minutes or increase by 80% the high-quality decisions that occur in a 2-hour meeting.

But you might.

CHAPTER 54

What Is The Risk?

Life On The Wire

Do you remember the high wire circus act of the Flying Wallendas? They were a family famous for their seven-person pyramid performed without a net. The net creates, Karl Wallenda, the father, said, a false sense of security. For years they had mesmerized, enthralled. No net. Perfect balance.

One day in Wisconsin at the Barnum and Bailey Circus, the front man faltered, and the pyramid collapsed. Karl Wallenda crashed to the ground, his hips and legs breaking. Others did, too. Three hung from the wire until a net could be dragged in and secured. They dropped to safety.

Later a reporter (the then very young Scott Simon now famously of NPR) interviewed Karl Wallenda. Scott asked him, "Mr Wallenda, will you ever go back up on the wire?"

Mr Wallenda looked Scott straight in the eyes. He paused. He said slowly, "Son, *life* is on the wire. All of the rest is waiting."

Scott Simon told that story 40 years later in a university commencement address. He said, "I knew in that moment that I wanted to live life on the wire."

His version of the wire has been anchoring news on TV and radio in front of millions of people worldwide. I imagine that his 16-hour coverage on September 11th was the highest wire of all for him.

Those two life-on-the-wire examples are dramatic. The risk grabs your throat. I have never done anything that visibly perilous. But I think I know what Karl and Scott meant. In a certain way every minute of creating a Thinking Environment is life on the wire. And the decision truly to be a presence that helps people think for themselves is a decision to say no to the net. I am sure Martin Kalungu-Banda also would agree, looking back on those 36 minutes when his whole country's welfare depended on the efficacy of a Thinking Environment, and his President's (and his own) courage to sustain it.

Life on the wire is the meaning, challenge and true self-expression most people say they long for. But most people look up at the wire, consider it and say no. Something backs them off. I think it is the perceived risk. I suspect it is that need for certainty. But, as Scott also said, and as Karl implied, with the right level of skill, there is no inevitable risk in living on the wire. The risk is in deciding not to.

Life on the wire requires supreme presence. It is life at its highest capacity to respond accurately to this very second and to all its differences from the second before. It is life at its most whole and alert and centred.

And, strangely, only when we are this present is there no danger. The Wallendas' pyramid collapsed when one person stopped being present to the requirements of that second. This is just as true of driving, and of chopping wood, injecting Thiopental, fingering the waste disposal, targeting your anger or eating sugar.

People feel they need to know what to do in case the person says or thinks something they can't predict. They don't listen because they are frightened to venture into territory they cannot control. And you know what is wrong with that concept? We will never know what we should do when something happens we cannot predict. That is why we have a brain. It was made especially for dealing with this single fact of life: Every moment is new. Our brains are custom-made to interact with the never-before. That is what truly good thinking is.

And the funny thing about all of this risk aversion in the presence of another's mind is that it risks only the demise of habit, not of anything valuable. In fact, it is exactly the prevention of fresh thinking, and the canned responses, always out of date, that are risky. They are dangerous. Dangerous, not as in the Wallendas without a net or Scott Simon without a script. Truly dangerous. As in slaying the human mind and its potential to create rich human experiences and amazing new social and economic systems that will mean a good life for everyone on the planet, and unleash beauty that will make our cores dance. That kind of dangerous.

Wallenda loved the wire not because of its risk to life, but because of what it demanded from him. It was in those microseconds of trust and decision that real living lay. It was the edge, not of the wire itself, but of the possibility, of his ability to calculate and re-calculate and to provide the exact right environment for the six others to do that, too.

For Scott, too, the wire was the requirement that he have to think, that he have to calibrate and re-calibrate, notice exactly what was happening in the moment and interact with that, not with a flat-pack reality. Could he create in the middle of catastrophe, as he said was his goal, both the understanding of unspeakable loss, and the fact that there would be a tomorrow, and after that another tomorrow? Could he? Could he be so present, so alert, so engaged, so eager to think well about the next new moment that he could hold the balance?

That is what we are doing when we stand before another human mind thinking for itself. When we want to know what the person truly does think, and when we know that in response we, too, can think, for ourselves, afresh, we know we do not need to be afraid.

I think that the challenge before us in this century is to choose life on the wire, to choose to create environments in which people can think for themselves.

Karl and Scott reflect the way it feels to be impeccably present with people and to plumb for a person's *own* thinking, even when it is tempting to make them salivate for ours.

When we want the human mind in front of us to unfold before us so much more than we want to protect ourselves from the unpredictability

Part Three

In Progress

CHAPTER 55

How Wide Is The Sky?

Five Forays For The Future

This geography, internal and external, is big. It is bountiful. It is hearty. The Thinking Environment seems to be the way human beings at their best prefer to do things. Especially when intelligent change is their passion.

Here I would like to tell you about five such forays. They are as different from each other as topography can create. Equally, they are held trustworthily by a common seabed.

Their infrastructures, the Ten Components of a Thinking Environment, also need just about the same degree of intelligent care as does our earth.

And as from the earth, life emerges from them – life that is an accurate symbiosis of thinking and feeling.

So let's start with, because it thematically segues into, Jamie and Sara, and the giant subject of "sustainability" and "enough". They have made it very personal.

CHAPTER 56

How Will You Know?

Sustainability And The Sign Of Enough

I read a health test question. It alarmed me. The article first said: "Describe your current life – the number of hours you sleep each night; the amount of time you rush; the proportion of your day you worry; the amount of time you don't just sit; the amount of time you don't listen to your children and your partner; the amount of time people don't listen to you; the amount of time you complain; the amount of self-betrayal you do by not sticking to your value of self-care; the amount of time you do emails; the amount of the day you don't exercise; the number of days per month you drink alcohol; how often you don't laugh; how frequently you don't eat freshly prepared food; your waist measurement; your weight; the amount of time you spend in airplanes and cars; the amount of time you are away from the people you love the most."

And here was the scary question: "Is this sustainable?"

Not all of those issues applied to me, but some did and they were big, and in the skinniest flash I knew the answer. No, this is not sustainable.

These days the word "sustainable" is both abstract and overused. We are all for it, but we have no real idea what it means. And we are not all for it if it applies too rigourously to our very specific selves. We have our fingers in our ears as it walks by. The word "deadly," however, is not abstract. It gets our attention. And that is the word, in invisible ink, that drips through the question: "Is this sustainable?"

In the face of that question, I faced some things and made some changes. I am proud of that. But I am each day still slow at letting in the question, because for almost all of us, it usually dictates the dismantling of denial. And then change. Now.

Jamie Armstrong really gets this. He sat me down a few years ago with his laptop, a bit of clever software and his impeccable Attention and Thinking Environment skill. And he asked me some fantastic questions. The questions emerged from four grids, four areas of focus on sustainability. He asked me about my body, my money, my interface with the physical environment and my relationships. And he listened as if I were the smartest person on the planet.

And then he did some whizzo things with colour and numbers and lines on the screen; and, shocked, I understood truly how unsustainable most of my four areas of life were. Equally important, I felt good about the bits that were sustainable. And best of all he helped me do my own thinking about how positively to progress my sustainable patterns, and how to stop or change the others. I felt good at the end. And I feel good now because day by day the green lines are definitely overtaking the red.

I think this sustainability coaching process is one of the most important things going on in the world. If we all did it, and then made the changes in the way we live, we would contribute impressively to a future of humanity as well as a good future for ourselves.

There is one other thing about the question, "Is it sustainable?" Non-thinking Environments are not. Thinking Environments are. Cultures of interruption, domination, criticism, stoicism, lies, denial, competition, urgency, humiliation, sameness of identity and thought and immersion in untrue limiting assumptions cannot go on forever – people suffer and die in them (and from them) sometimes physically, always spiritually. Or they leave if they can. And the quality of decision-making in them leads to systems and policies that are themselves unsustainable. And also kill.

But cultures of Attention, Equality, Ease, Appreciation, Information, Encouragement, Feelings, Diversity of identity and thought, Incisive Questions and Places that say, "You matter", can go on and on, forever.

Only sustainable – and good – things come from them.

So, if leaders and managers and teachers and politicians were to take seriously the question, "Is this sustainable?" and heed its answers, something else would happen, too. Pretty soon we all would, I think, begin to ask some big, serious questions.

The Sign Of Enough

One of the biggest would be, "How much is enough?"

This is where Sara comes in. (I know she came in also in the Facilitation chapter, but I can't help how talented she is.) Sara Hart has been asking that question for nearly a decade. She has created *The Sign of Enough*, and a workshop in which people address that question from several angles. Sara is clear: "Enough" is a creative concept. It is completely consistent with ongoing innovation, entrepreneurial enterprise and individual initiative. She is also clear that we need right this minute to think hard about it. And let it change our lives.

She also thinks we have to create a Thinking Environment to make this thinking happen well. And I am clear that when we do, sustainable, big, big, big (good) things are going to happen. Whole systems, not just individual lives (though certainly those, too), are going to change.

Sara knows this. In her workshops people learn just enough about the Ten Components and practice just enough of the skill of thinking in pairs and in Rounds, and the skill of building Incisive Questions to be able to get their authentic minds around some questions in reference to chewy areas of their lives (such as money, power, food, love, ambition, friends, things, control, appreciation, fame, security, time).

How much is enough?

How will you know when you have enough?

What are you assuming that keeps you from knowing how much is enough?

If you were to strive for enough and not for more, what would you do with the excess?

If you knew that enough is good, what change would you make?

When?

America rarely asks itself, "What is enough?" Britain doesn't either. And neither does China. In fact, our global economic system itself doesn't, can't, ask itself that question. It hates the question. After all, if we get interested in what enough is, however enlightening some of the answers may be, it may be that we give up greed. It may be that we *actually* face the fact that some people have way too much, and that that is because more people have way too little, and that all of that does not, and never has had, to do with how hard people work, or how intelligent they are.

If we figure out what enough is, we may find ourselves wanting to answer this question:

If we knew that we are intelligent enough to figure out a new system of economics that produces motivated, creative individuals and organizations, high levels of innovation, and more than enough money and well-being for every single person on the planet, what might the key features of this new system be?

We probably would have to look soberly at our untrue limiting assumptions in order to do this extraordinary degree of new thinking. And we certainly would have to set up the Ten Components as our framework for being together while we think about this. We would, absolutely and first, have to listen like mad and take equal turns.

Anyway, the thing about Sara is that she is herself so completely non-judgemental, you can think about these questions, come up with some concrete answers, decide what to change and change it, without ever needing to defend the indefensible.

Guilt doesn't feature, either, with her. The Thinking Environment she creates is genuine, organic, a way of being. And so these iconoclastic sojourns are nearly always transformative and practical.

Maybe Jamie and Sara should get together. Maybe it is time, at long last, for Sustainability and the Sign of Enough to be centre stage in a very bright light.

And with no final curtain.

CHAPTER 57

Who Is The Expert?

The Professional In A Thinking Environment

I remember in 1970 seeing a book on a friend's desk. The title was: *Can You Trust Your Experts?* For 265 pages the answer was no.

I agreed and went on my way. Over the years I shook hands with the few experts I had to meet, scepticism and deep-breathing being sufficient to get me through. Mostly I stayed away from them.

Until I met Scott Farnsworth. (I can't help how talented he is, either.) Now, Scott is a man of remarkable innovation, anyway. But as an estate-planning and legacy advisor (and now teacher of advisors) he is disarmingly cutting-edge. He thinks that professionals should be humble. He thinks they should want to hear what their clients think. And he thinks clients' stories are everything.

Scott called me one day in 2003. It was my birthday. I had decided I would do no work at all that day, nor make any plans because it was also the one-year anniversary of my twin brother's funeral. I wanted to let the day find its own way. I also wanted cake and ice cream in our favourite flavours. My heart was still hurting.

But Scott's email a few days before had caught my imagination. So I said, "I am intrigued." And he called.

He told me about SunBridge, his network of estate-planning advisors who are learning how to be with their clients in such a way that the clients figure out what really matters to them, and along the way tell the stories of their lives, their values, their dreams and accomplishments. The advisor can then create an estate plan that exactly reflects the client, capturing the stories themselves as part of a legacy of intangible wealth, as well as money. I had never heard of this before. I just barely had a will.

And I remembered my Dad during his lunch at home, (he came home for lunch every day, and then had a 30-minute nap; why didn't I learn that from him?) collapsing on the sofa one day when I was about ten. He said, exhaling, "It is too expensive to die." I thought he meant the price of coffins. I started to cry. How did I know he was talking about inheritance tax?

I had not progressed much beyond that naivety 45 years later when Scott called.

He had read my book. He said it had become required reading for his programme. He said he had been on Rick Stone's Thinking Partnership Programme. He loved it. He asked if I would come to Orlando to speak to his network.

He also said he was born and raised in New Mexico and that his birthday was in May. And he was left-handed. By then I figured this call was organized by the higher-ups. I was, of course, also thrilled to hear about his application of the Ten Components. The very idea that professional advisors of any kind, especially lawyers, especially in America, would embrace the challenge of establishing equality with their clients was more a celebration than cake and ice cream.

So in November I went to Orlando. And over these years since then I have watched SunBridge and the National Network and other interlocking networks of estate advisors consider the possibility that the client has the answers. No matter what law school said. The client's answers are the important ones. The technical bits slot in. Not the other way around.

So there it was again, the "expert" issue. This time the question was not, "Can you trust your experts?" It was more fundamental than that. It was, "Who *is* the expert?"

Let's say you are the advisor. And for "advisor" read: Lawyer, doctor, accountant, teacher, counsellor, psychologist, coach, decorator, consultant, seismologist – you name it. Whatever it is, you, the advisor, have expertise. Lots of it. You studied for it, paid for it, developed it, have been honoured and rewarded for it. You charge for it. You and your clients rely on it.

Your obvious expertise is transactional: Financial, technical, legal, structural, psychological, practical knowledge.

But there is a not-so-obvious expertise your clients want from you. It is the ability *to be a Thinking Environment* for them. They want this. They may not know they want it; but they do. They will choose you over other advisors if you provide it. They may not know why, but they will. They want to think for themselves.

They want to figure things out, say things, discover things, create things they have never had access to before. They want to be asked. They want to be listened to, impeccably.

But when they make their first appointment, they do not tell you that this expertise is more important to them than all the rest. They think they are supposed to want only the technical stuff.

So when your client enters your office, it is vital to remember that there are now *two* experts in the room. You know your field, and they know their life.

Rick Randall of the National Network, another group of vanguard estate planners, also understands this expert issue. Their version of it is "The Planning Pyramid." And the Network's commitment to becoming a Thinking Environment is apparently bringing the Pyramid to life at a new level now.

Knowing this, you can practise this way. From the minute your clients walk into your office, you can create a Thinking Environment for them. When you do, you as the expert in the Thinking Environment liberate the expert in them.

Creating a Thinking Environment for your clients, regardless of their level of net worth, so that they can *think for themselves* about both the technical and the transcendent aspects of planning is to catalyse two kinds of expertise into a life-changing experience. And the result is a plan, an outcome, of much greater value.

Once I got over the surprise of seeing lawyers peel themselves away from the need to be the only expert, and become more and more expert in drawing out the expert in their clients, I began to wonder what it would be like for doctors to behave this way. I wondered how it would be for us as patients if doctors truly recognized the expert in us. How much more accurate could their diagnoses be, and how much more accurate and inclusive would their prescriptions for healing become, if they could embody the Ten Components in every consultation with every patient?

I thought of Jerome Groopman's book, *How Doctors Think*, and of his breakthrough point that the patient is the expert and that doctors need to listen deeply and long to them. Accurate diagnosis and treatment absolutely depend on it.

They need to stop listening to diagnose, and start listening to understand.

I thought of Ignaz Semmelweiss. It took him more than all of his 19th-century life to convince fellow doctors to wash their hands before doing surgery and delivering babies. To wash them thoroughly. I wonder how long it may take Dr Groopman to convince fellow doctors to listen before delivering diagnoses. To listen thoroughly.

I wonder, in fact, what might happen if the first experts – parents – and the second experts – teachers – could see themselves as only one of the experts in their relationship with young people. And I wonder how much better professionals those young people would become themselves as a result.

The last Christmas morning my Mother was alive, she was sitting at one end of the long sofa. I was sitting at the other. Quiet was always easy between us. And out of our quiet a question usually emerged that took us down wonderful roads. On this day, frail, she nevertheless spoke clearly, her voice still deep and resonant. She spoke slowly. "Honey, there is something I would like to ask you."

She paused and looked at me. She was both far away and wholly present. She spoke deliberately, warmly.

"What would you like to accomplish with the rest of *your* life?"

I think I was startled. I was startled by the clean lines of it. And by its boldness. And its generosity. I did not answer right at first. I remember thinking that I wanted to answer as an adult. An adult on the inside. It did not matter that I was 38 on the outside. I felt 12. And I wanted to grow completely up in that moment.

I wanted to honour her with the truth. I wanted not to think for a second about what she might want me to say, or what might please her. I also wanted to answer her question with serenity. And I wanted to step across the sadness that sat between us, the knowing that she was dying, but the refusing to know, too.

I said, "I want to make a difference. I think that poor thinking lies at the heart of what is wrong with the world. So I want to help people think for themselves well. And maybe if people started thinking for themselves, they would ask better questions, too. I agree with whoever said that the answer is only as good as the question."

I drew breath. I had said it, exactly, even if it started to sound a little teachy at the end. I smiled. So did she, her respect penetrating. There was another comfortable silence.

Then tenderly she asked me, "And how do you hope to achieve this?"

Startled again, again I decided to think clearly and speak the truth. Even if it might seem naive. I did not have a plan exactly yet. But instead of making one up on the spot, I just said what I really thought.

"I hope to step back from all I have learned and read in my life, and discovered at our school, and ask, as if for the first time, the question: What *does* it take for people to think for themselves?

"And then I want to gather people together to do their own thinking about things important to them. Over time I hope to observe afresh what needs to happen to keep them thinking. I have decided not to be afraid of being proved wrong. I know this will take time, and I have no idea what kind of living I can make from it, but that's what I hope to do."

I breathed. And she said, "Well, honey, that is a wonderful thing to do with your life, and if you do it just the way you have said, you may do something really valuable."

I wanted to cry. Mostly, I think, from how big the moment had been. How indelible. And also from wondering how she knew to ask me those questions.

That also puzzled my colleague 23 years later. David Cohn was driving me to the Denver airport. I had asked David about his work with family systems and the complexities of helping families who own large family businesses plan their estates and legacies. And he had asked me about my life's journey. For some reason I told him that story of Mother's questions.

His response startled me as surely as Mother's questions had. "Do you know how extraordinary your mother's questions were?" he asked me. I kept listening.

"It is the question all parents should be asking their children. And it is exactly the question parents don't ask. They are often too frightened to hear the answers. They are frightened because they want their children to want to do what they want them to do, the thing that defines success in *their* minds.

"Families fracture because your mother's question is not even on the table. And certainly her respect for your authentic answer is not on the table. Her ability to listen to you, her desire to know what *you* were thinking, and then generously and succinctly and selflessly to affirm you is on hardly any table in any family anywhere.

"In my work I try to help families ask questions like your mother's. I also try to teach them to do what your mother did naturally: to *want* to know what their children really think and want, and to see their children as more important than the business. And then to plan and to build the business on truth."

We reached the fanciful floating concrete canopy that is the Denver airport, and I appreciated him, both for his work and for showing me how easy it is, even in one's last moments on earth, to shape a life. And how important it is to do it so that that life shapes itself.

So I think Scott, and his colleagues, are really on to something big.

And here is a little something to laminate and put on your blotter. It might turn out to be your best friend, professionally speaking.

ADVISOR CHECKLIST
Read one minute before any client meeting

Remember

Being a Thinking Environment for your client is valuable expertise.

Your client wants your advice. But more than that they want to think for themselves.

They want to be listened to without interruption.

The value you offer your client increases with every minute you listen to them.

Your client's thinking will improve yours.

Your relationship with your client is a partnership, not a performance.

You are both expert.

Do

Get interested in what your client thinks, and will say next.

Don't interrupt or rush them as they speak.

Keep your eyes on their eyes, and your face welcoming.

Ask them what more they think, or feel or want to say.

Regard them as your equal.

Or maybe you could just memorize it.

Or better yet, just *be* it.

CHAPTER 58

Where Are You?

Email And Other Things Floating Around

This chapter is an act of rescue. And writing it is almost a civic duty. Let's start with email. However marvellous email is in obvious ways, it is a tyranny. No human being should have to receive a hundred or more communications (of any sort) in a day. Much less communications that by their nature demand instant response. Why there aren't more office suicides from all of this is a mystery.

The point here is that like a true bully, email, as it is usually done, keeps people from thinking. For one thing, people say the most appalling things in emails, things they would never have said in person, or even in a letter. It is as if the keyboard and the instantaneousness of the medium take a blow torch to our discretion and thoughtfulness, and cheer us on like sadists watching a dog fight, and we communicate as if our recipient had neither heart nor gut. Nor brain.

Emails for some reason make us stupid. As we write them, we don't notice the recipient. We don't listen. We don't register the second-by-second potential response. We don't then re-think to find a more intelligent, thoughtful way of saying the next sentence.

The importance of noticing, listening and re-thinking – essentials in intelligent behaviour – seems to escape us as we go into a kind of impact-coma the minute the message template appears and our fingers hop on the keyboard.

We fail to ask ourselves:

How will the recipient feel when they read this?

How might they misinterpret these words?

What might these words do to their self-esteem and their ability to think independently and respectfully in reply?

How do I listen to the recipient as if they were with me?

How do I write this so that the recipient can think well as they read it?

How can I appreciate them in this message?

These are questions that just do not occur to us as we write emails. But they are questions that would occur to us if we were speaking in person, and probably even if we were writing a hard-copy letter. (At least, I hope they would.)

This psychic carnage really needs to stop. So how can we perform the miracle of turning our emails into Thinking Environments?

In one thrust, we can open up the list of the Ten Components and make sure they are all present before we press "send." That should help.

We also can make that job easier by picturing the person. We can "pull up a chair" for them. We can "look into their eyes" and remember that in front of us is a human being with an extraordinary, under-used human mind, and with a warm heart (inherently, at least). We can let them matter profoundly. Then we can write.

This will mean greeting them warmly and using their name. It will mean at the end saying goodbye warmly. Not taking forever. Just humanly, the way you would if they were sitting with you. In person you just would not start in on the issue without saying hello and looking at them, nor would you get up at the end of the conversation and turn away from them and start working on something else. In person we are more human. And when we are not, we notice it. Most of us, anyway. We can tell we have been unkind or dismissive. But in emails we pretend that disconnected, unaware-of-others behaviour is not happening, and that if it is, it does not matter.

The main thing to remember is that it *is* happening, and it does matter. However flash and sleek our virtual tools are, and however much they become more so, the human being is still there, wanting to think and needing to be treated well in order to do that. The human being is the point. The rest is support. And when that support actually hacks up some of the point, we need to back up, sit down for a second and think about what we are doing. And then do it differently.

So I don't think that email in a Thinking Environment is an oxymoron. But I do think it is a decision – to notice, to care and to keep the human being on the other end of the mail thinking beautifully. We have to care about that.

Which brings me to another thought. How virtual can things get and still produce the best of human beings? Can we have high-quality relationships at work across continents with people whom we never greet with the warmth of skin and eyes? Can we message, but not touch – and still know each other? Can we think well enough together when we are never together?

We have to. At least part of the time. This is where society is headed. Talk with Nicola Strong about this. She knows what it is going to take to keep the human being human in a virtual, remote world. She will relax you on the subject and make you laugh, and she will dignify you and make you think, and you will leave (or exit) feeling promisingly competent and relieved and fascinated.

Nicola is pioneering virtual meetings in a Thinking Environment. And she is discovering about remote working and building of teams that, "advanced technology can work in a Thinking Environment, and without the Thinking Environment technology does not work."

Nicola thinks of it this way: Remote + Thinking Environment = Presence.

She sees it as an equation that can free the human mind and heart, really.

So, as with all interactions, I guess we just need to ask ourselves the question: How do I help this human being in front of me, in person or on line, to think for themselves well? And then we need to do it.

I hope I live until 2030, and that Nicola does, too. I want to see how much positive influence she and the Thinking Environment can have over the way real human beings create reality.

CHAPTER 59

Why Do They Leave?

Living Your Values

How much did your organization spend figuring out its values? And how much did it cost to get it inscribed in granite, or plexiglass or at least in a three-colour brochure?

See if you can get a refund. I don't want to be brutal here, but statistically speaking you have just created a document that will be the source of one of the top five greatest reasons for contempt, de-motivation, disloyalty and turnover in your organization. All of this from the discrepancy between the values on the wall and the values on the ground.

Organizations list values. But they don't live them. And people hate that. They really, really hate it. They would rather not have organizational values than to see leaders live their opposites.

Most consultants get those senior teams to come up with the values, but they don't get them to embody them. The organization pays a lot for the consultant. But it pays a lot more, and a lot longer, for the hypocrisy.

Some organizations, of course, are aware of this. Maybe yours is one of them. Maybe you have worked into appraisals, for example, an assessment of how the person is demonstrating the organization's values. Maybe you have defined team success as concretely embodying the corporate values in the way you manage people or relate to customers, and even maybe in the products you design and sell. This is good.

But if not, or maybe even if so, consider a fire-proof way to determine just exactly how truly to live organizational values. A non-profit executive team wanted to do this. So they started by placing in front of themselves the list of their organizational values. It was:

People

Communication

Partnership

Creativity

Open management

Diversity

Community involvement

Fairness

Look familiar? You might consider creating a new revenue stream by selling your values list to other organizations, and save them a lot of time. But, of course, it matters that the list be generated by the people themselves. All 12 of them. Which is part of the problem. The values are hardly ever generated by the people, as in *everyone*. So engaging everyone would be a good start even before tackling the living-them issue.

Anyway, this team then considered the living of the values from two perspectives: the individual and the organization. They answered these questions, and always in a Thinking Environment in Thinking Pairs, in Rounds, in open discussion, all with no interruption and with equal turns. (It did not escape their notice that this process in itself was an expression of seven of the eight values.)

They opened the day with these questions:

Which one of our eight values is most important to you personally?

What about it matters to you?

Which of the values do you think you live well enough now?

How does your behaviour demonstrate this value?

Then they reviewed their understanding that all values (good and bad actually) are driven by assumptions. They completed these statements around the group:

We value people because we assume that _____.

We value communication because we assume that _____.

We value partnership because we assume that _____.

And so forth....

And then they got to work, first from an individual perspective. They answered, first in pairs and then in Rounds, these questions:

Which of the eight values do you need to be living better?

How would you have to *behave* as a way of living that value better?

What might you be assuming that stops you from behaving that way?

What would you credibly have to assume in order to behave that way?

They then moved that liberating credible assumption into an Incisive Question:

If you knew that (insert liberating true assumption), how would you behave consistently?

What would be the benefits of that behaviour?

After lunch the focus was changed to the organization. The questions were:

Which of the eight values do you think the organization needs to live better?

How would the organization have to behave as a way of living that value better?

What is the organization assuming that is stopping it from behaving that way?

What would the organization have to assume in order to behave that way?

If all of the organization knew that (insert liberating true assumption), how would it behave consistently?

What would be the concrete benefits of that behaviour?

It was a stimulating day. And a review later showed greater trust among the staff of the executive team, and among themselves a greater sense of being valued.

But let's re-think this a moment. Let's consider this question: If you are not living the organization's values, what values are you living? Leaders who don't live the organization's values, are still living values. But they are living other values. If they don't live people, they live objects. If they don't live communication, they live manipulation. If they don't live creativity, they live status quo. If they don't live open management, they live control. If they don't live diversity, they live conformity. If they don't live community involvement, they live detachment. If they don't live fairness, they live exploitation.

People are made furious not so much by the values the leaders are *not* living, but by the ones they are living instead. And they are furious in the face of the assumptions that drive those other values.

The assumptions demean, dishearten, dismiss and discourage people.

And that is why digging down to come up with Incisive Questions that lead to living the corporate values consistently is consistently a good idea.

We are always living values. Let's just be sure we value the values we are living.

CHAPTER 60

Whose Future Is It?

Thinking In South Africa

*I am human because I belong. My humanity is
inextricably bound up in yours.*

*I am open and available to you, affirming of you. I do
not feel threatened that you are able and good. I have
a proper self-assurance that comes from knowing that I
belong in a greater whole and am diminished when you
are diminished, when you are humiliated or treated as if
you were less than who you are.*

This is *Ubuntu*. The concept that we are one. And in that one-ness we are
individuals, honoured. And in our individuality we honour each other.

I first heard the word "Ubuntu" from Lesedi Makhurame. We were in
Cape Town in the middle of our ever-unfolding conversation about the
potential impact of the Ten Components of a Thinking Environment on
society. He changed my life, as he does many others', and this time by
sharing, and being, Ubuntu. A year later I read the above adapted words
in Desmond Tutu's book, *No Future Without Forgiveness*.

Ubuntu holds for us all the greatest of all challenges: To live each
moment aware of our impact on each other, and to want that to be
only good.

Margaret Legum, 30 years after writing *South Africa: Crisis For The
West*, at the request of Mandela, calling for economic sanctions against

apartheid, said to me, "The Thinking Environment may be essential for real transformation in South Africa. I want to teach it and get it into common practice, make it a way of being."

Margaret did teach it, in townships and boardrooms and women's groups and business schools – everywhere she could. And just before her tragic death in November 2007, she saw promising Thinking Environment competence emerging. This growth comes from her understanding of change.

The whole of her dream will take longer than she had here. And of course it requires multiple overlapping developments. It will probably in the end be systems born of Ubuntu that create a world that is good, truly good, for everyone. Not trickle-down good, not good-for-the-already-fine-minority-but-that's-all, not good-for-all-three-centuries-from-now. But good now, for all. And that is because the idea that some people are better than others sits like radium in the roots of the systems that produce huge differentials of wealth and power. It sits there, burning us. Disfiguring our decisions. Some-people-are-better-than-others drives what isn't working.

And it is not good enough to say that what we have now is better than anything else human beings have tried. It probably is, overall. But better-than just does not have anything to do with good.

Ubuntu is the reference point. It is also the starting point. And it is the goal. It is the Incisive Question:

If you knew that our humanity is inextricably bound up in each other, what systemic changes would you make in our society?

We will have to start with Ubuntu if we are going to find our way to a new place that works. A place that is good, not just better than the bad.

I think that what Margaret knew was that new systems will come from new thinking and that new thinking will come from Thinking Environments. From the gathering of human beings to listen in ways profound and easeful and wildly supportive. Ways with no interruption for sure. But also ways with brevity and focus because we want to know what the others think, because we are one and the same and different all at once. We need each other because we are each other. And if the systems don't work for you, they don't work for me.

I think Margaret also knew that narcissism shrivels in Ubuntu. Ubuntu ensures that maniacal urges sit out the conversation. The human under them is fine. The pathology isn't. Equal turns, no interruption, encouragement, feelings, information, appreciation and Incisive Questions all sprout from the seed of Ubuntu. Not from the stone of I.

Maybe you will be lucky enough to meet Lesedi. Or Isaac Matheta Swafo, Dorrian Hodge, Trisha Lord, Maryse Barak, Helena Dolny, Candice Smith-Abrahams, Sunny Stout-Rostron. And now others. They spend time with individuals and organizations creating Thinking Environments in order to explore and dismantle untrue assumptions about race, about positional power, about better-than-ness.

So, our hearts can take heart.

For a while. When the leaders participate, the while gets longer. And when the leaders see, for example, the disconnect between compliance with equity laws, and the embedded-so-invisible assumptions of better-than-you, the while has a real chance of being longer enough to fire up systemic change. The Thinking Environment may contribute to the living of Ubuntu. But Africans living consistent with Ubuntu discovered the Thinking Environment millennia ago.

Laws alone won't make Ubuntu the universal culture. Economics as we practise it won't do it; smiles on top of untrue limiting assumptions about each other won't do it; greed, in *anyone*, won't do it. What will do it is our freshness of thinking born of our burning need to live in the knowledge that we are nothing without each other.

It is my belief that South Africa, through many compatible processes, not just the Thinking Environment, and through thousands of determined ordinary leaders who live the concept of Ubuntu, will build on the historically unprecedented brilliance of Mandela and Tutu. They will continue to forge forward where fear before had forbidden entrance.

And the rest of us will see what we already know: we are one. And a no-net, high-wire one at that.

Part Three

In The End

CHAPTER 61

How Will It End?

The Promise Of Paradox

I believe that it is possible for the world to become a Thinking Environment. Human beings long for it. We are born, I think, expecting it. We wake everyday hoping, however vaguely, that today, finally, we will be asked what we think and then be listened to without interruption, and then appreciated. We are, I think, on every journey home from work disappointed when that did not happen. But we hope, somewhere in our most intelligent heart, that tomorrow it just might.

We also hope each day that we will have a significant impact on others, that we will find a way to free each other from the invisible but teeth-bearing grip our untrue limiting assumptions have on our lives. We don't word it that way; we don't perhaps even know quite what the longing is. But it is there. And it tugs at the sleeves of our days, begging to be noticed.

And when we see it, when someone treats us to a Thinking Environment, we rejoice. Maybe we tilt our heads at first and frown, puzzled. Maybe we say, "Humph," at first. Some of us do.

But this is nearly always a way of saying, "Please don't be wrong about this. Please let it be possible that life and love and learning and debate and decision-making and growing and creating and just being can be this good. For real. Forever."

I think there is such a hard-wired desire for this much quality and diversity and respect, and for the very real results that spring from them that people will, when it is offered sensitively, say, "Thank you.

Why have we lived otherwise for so long?"

But what if we should hesitate? What if we should continue to postpone the moment? What if we should continue to allow lives to spread like rawhide, rather than undulate and soar?

Perhaps we would turn to the poets. Often it is the poets who tell us the truth so that we can hear it.

TS Eliot and Davison Budhoo are two. Both suggest that to embrace the chance to move the world toward its true heart, we must first embrace paradox. Paradox, they say, is inside the mystery of life. Paradox is also the heart of the Thinking Environment. We have already seen how central to our creating of Thinking Environments is our comfort with paradox. Consider these:

As the Thinking Partner you are both essential
and irrelevant.

You matter profoundly because you do not matter at all.

You are so present you become invisible.

You are still in order to be productive.

You question in order to trust.

You risk in order to be safe.

Doing means not doing.

The brain that contains the question usually contains
the answer.

In a hierarchy people are equals.

Freedom requires boundaries.

A Thinking Environment turns no time into more time.

Expressing feelings is a rational act.

The greater the diversity of thinking, the greater the unity of decision.

We want to be wrong in order to get closer to being right.

Slowing down speeds things up.

These contradictions generate the power of the Thinking Environment. In his poem "Little Gidding" from *The Four Quartets*, Eliot seems to understand this. He helps us see the ultimate paradox, that life's end and life's beginning are the same thing, and not the same at all.

In a Thinking Session we see this, too. We know that thinking and listening are not linear; they are creation. We know, as Eliot shows us beautifully, that it is precisely the thinker's words that matter, and that we are there only for a privileged moment, not sculpting the start nor fashioning the finish, not knowing for certain which is which, reverent throughout.

I hope you will find "Little Gidding" and read it afresh with the paradoxes of a Thinking Environment in mind.

Davison Budhoo, too, takes us into the certainty of uncertainty, the end that is the beginning, the belonging that is the separation. And we see here a metaphor for the paradox-rich injunction to think for yourself:

At some stage, said the Northern Star,
You must stop the pre-arranged reel,
However interesting it may be,
However titillating to the Gods.
Stop it and take potluck.
Face your audience head on, without props,
Without supporting cast, without rehearsal,
Throw your soul at their feet, and make them

Either to trample on it,

Or to embrace it into themselves.

In the waxing and waning of your tide

There is a knowledge awaiting discovery–

A knowledge never learnt,

Nor even sought before,

Because it is too disturbing for

Humankind. If you can find that knowledge, use it wisely

To make your world compassionate.

Use it tonight, unapologetically,

Before your time runs out.

It is the ultimate present presence. It is the generating and unfolding of intelligence.

I believe we are ready for paradox.

I believe we are ready for this much life.

Appendices And Bibliography

Good Question

These seven questions are worth keeping in your pocket. They aren't as perfect as custom-made Incisive Questions, but they will wake you up:

Then what?

What is the question?

What do you think?

What do you know now, that you are going to find out in a year?

If it were entirely up to you, how would you improve this situation?

What is enough?

How will you know when you have it?

Researching The Thinking Environment

I

EMILY HAVERS

emilyhavers@btinternet.com

A Study of Whether and How Meetings in a Thinking Environment Impact Organizational Life

University of Southampton, United Kingdom, 2009

Emily Havers conducted research into the effectiveness of the Transforming Meetings Programme. This study interviewed 15 senior officers from 11 organizations on 3 continents.

> Organizations are now aware of the need to unlock the unique potential within each individual at work in order to be successful in the new knowledge age.
>
> Leading researchers in the field note that a focus on enhancing how people think, rather than what people do, is very different from conventional organizational development practice. This study came up with significant findings in the efficacy of holding meetings in a Thinking Environment as an approach that generates people's best thinking.

It found a 95% consistency in the outcomes of meetings held in a Thinking Environment, including that these meetings time and again:

Produced a measurable, positive impact on the performance indicators of organizations

Generated better ideas, solutions and decisions

Created an environment in which people felt valued and equal

Achieved resolution faster

Gave rise to greater participation and more involvement from everyone

Fostered productive working relationships

"There is absolutely no doubt in my mind that these meetings have produced the best results of any meetings I've been in. It's been a total change. It's been a real eye opener for me. I've been running meetings for years and years and years, and I've never experienced the feeling of success coming out of meetings that I've felt coming out of these meetings in a Thinking Environment."

Managing Director, insurance retail

"I can positively say that our business has improved by at least 20 percent. And that's measurable in financial terms."

Provincial Director, financial services

II

BEVERLY WHITEHEAD

beverly.whitehead@careerstory.co.za

Newlands Brewery Pilot Mentoring Programme Cape Town, South Africa 2007

Beverly Whitehead conducted research into the effectiveness of the Time To Think Mentoring Programme. After six months working with sixteen mentoring pairs, Beverly's organization reported benefits not only for the mentees, but also for the organization.

The sixteen interviewees described their experience as:

Powerful

Mutually beneficial

Eye opening

Synergistic with the leadership brand and with the leadership essentials

Transferable into other contexts

Beneficial to our non-mentoring relationship with one another

A majority reported that the programme:

Balanced the voices in the organization

Increased respect for each other

Developed interpersonal skills

And that through it people:

Shared knowledge and experience

Generated good thinking, ideas and innovation

Solved work problems

Resolved inner conflicts relating to self or career

Bibliography

Arbinger Institute (2002) *Leadership and Self Deception*. San Francisco: Berrett-Koehler Publishers.

Arbinger Institute (2006) *The Anatomy of Peace*. San Francisco: Berrett-Koehler Publishers.

Bloom, H. (2000) *Global Brain: The Evolution of Mass Mind*. New York: John Wiley & Sons.

Brown, P. T. (2008) *Emerging Neuro-Sciences, Relationships and the Business of Coaching*. Henley: Association For Professional Executive Coaching and Supervision.

Bryson, B. (2004) *A Short History of Nearly Everything*. London: Random House.

Carroll, M. & Gilbert, M. (2005-2009) *Becoming an Executive Coachee: Creating Learning Partnerships*. West Ealing: Vukani Publishing.

de Haan, E. (2008) *Relational Coaching*. Chichester: John Wiley & Sons.

Dawkins, R. (2008) *The Oxford Book of Modern Science Writing*. Oxford: Oxford University Press.

Dolny, H., editor (2009) *Team Coaching: Artists At Work*. Johannesburg: Penguin.

Downey, Myles (2003) *Effective Coaching: Lessons From the Coach's Coach*. Mason: Thomson.

Dowrick, S. (1994) *Intimacy and Solitude*. New York and London: W. W. Norton.

Farnsworth, S & Hoyt, P. (2008) *Like a Library Burning*. Ovieda: Legacy Planning Partners.

Farnsworth, S. (2003) *Closing the Gap*. Orlando: SunBridge.

Feynman, R. (2007) *What Do You Care What Other People Think?* London: Penguin.

Feynman, R. (2005) *Don't You Have Time To Think?* London: Penguin.

Ford, B. (2002) *High Energy Habits*. London: Simon and Schuster.

Gallway, T. (1986) *The Inner Game of Tennis*. New York: Pan Macmillan.

Gerhardt, S. (2004) *Why Love Matters*. London: Routledge.

Glickstein, L. (1996) *Be Heard Now*. San Francisco: Leeway Press.

Gottman, J. M. & D. J. (2001) *The Relationship Cure*, New York: Crown Publishing.

Graessle, L., Gawlinski, G., & Farrell, M. (2006) *Meeting Together*. London: Graham Irwin.

Grayling, A.C. (2007) *The Mystery of Things: Life and What It Means*. London: Phoenix.

Groopman, J. (2007) *How Doctors Think*. New York: Houghton Mifflin.

Hardingham, A., Brearley, M., Moorhouse, A., Venter, B. (2004) *The Coach's Coach, Personal Development for Personal Developers*. London: CIPD Publishing.

Hawken, P. (1993) *The Ecology of Commerce: A Declaration of Sustainability*. New York: HarperCollins.

Hawkins, P. & Smith, N. (2008) *Coaching, Mentoring and Organizational Consultancy Supervision and Development*. Maidenhead: Open University Press.

Hobson, P. (2002) *Cradle Of Thought*. London: Pan Macmillan.

Hock, D. (2005). *One From Many: VISA and the Rise of Chaordic Organization*. San Francisco: Berrett-Koehler Publishers.

Isaacs, W. (1999) *Dialogue, The Art of Thinking Together*. New York: Doubleday.

Kline, N. (1993) *Women and Power: How Far Can We Go?* London: BBC Worldwide.

Kline, N. (1999) *Time To Think: Listening To Ignite the Human Mind*. London: Cassell.

Kline, N. & Spence, C. (1993) *At Least A Hundred Principles Of Love*. London: LLMS.

Kline, P. (2002) *Why America's Children Can't Think*. Maui: Inner Ocean Publishing.

Legum, M. (2002) *It Doesn't Have To Be Like This*. Kennilworth: Ampersand Press.

Lehrer, J. (2009) *The Decisive Moment: How the Brain Makes Up Its Mind*. London: Canongate.

Lewis, T., Amini, R., Lannon, F. (2001) *A General Theory Of Love*. New York: Random House.

Lowen, A. (1997) *Narcissism: Denial of the True Self*. New York: Touchstone.

Marsh, N (2007) *Observations of a Very Short Man*. New South Wales: Allen & Unwin.

McCraty, R. & Childre, D. (2002) *The Appreciative Heart: The Psychophysiology of Positive Emotions and Optimal Functioning*. Publication No. 02–026. San Francisco: The HeartMath Research Center, Institute of HeartMath.

Miller, A. (1986) *Thou Shalt Not Be Aware: Society's Betrayal of the Child*. New York: Meridian.

Nelson, N., Daniel A. & J., & Lemare, C. (2006) *The Power of Appreciation*. Malibu: Mindlab Publishing.

Obama, B. (2007) *Dreams From My Father*. London: Canongate.

Pink, D. (2008) *A Whole New Mind*. London: Marshall Cavendish.

Spence, C. (1996) *On Watch: Views From the Lighthouse*. London: Cassell.

Stout-Rostron, S. (2009) *Business Coaching Wisdom and Practice:*

Unlocking the Secrets of Business Coaching. Randburg: Knowres Publishing.

Taleb, N. (2007) *The Black Swan: The Impact of the Highly Improbable.* London: Penguin.

Temoshok, L. et al. (1990) *Psychosocial Perspectives On Aids: Etiology, Prevention, and Treatment.* London: Lawrence Erlbaum Associates Publishers.

Thomas, L. (1979) *The Medusa and the Snail.* New York: Penguin.

Thompson, M. (1991) *The Cry and the Covenant.* New York: Buccaneer Books.

Tutu, D. (2002) *No Future Without Forgiveness.* London: Rider.

Wilbur, K. (2006) *Integral Spirituality.* Boston: Shambhala.

Index

TIME
TO
THINK

LISTENING TO IGNITE
THE HUMAN MIND

"Do not be fooled by the simplicity of this process.
It will unleash the power of your whole organization."
British Telecom

NANCY KLINE

Living with
TIME TO
THINK
The goddaughter letters
Because they can think for themselves

'Every page is a gift ... offers timeless wisdom for us all'
Mark Williams, bestselling co-author of *Mindfulness*

NANCY KLINE